"Our firm is keenly focused on teaching our lawyers how to deepen relationships with clients through more thoughtful networking and relationship building. Mark's newest book fits perfectly with that goal and is the perfect tool in alignment with our values and culture. We intend to make this book available to every professional in our firm."

Pierre Paquet, Chair of National Business Development Committee,
Miller Thomson

"Mark Maraia has zeroed in on the essential component of successful selling — relationships. Our industry-leading sales force knows this. It is often said: It's not what you know, but whom you know. I believe it is both. By building strong relationships, we become trusted advisors to our clients, our associates, and our friends. They in turn confide in us. Mark outlines the importance of this symbiotic relationship and how to develop it in his book. It is a practical guide to relationship building."

Thomas C. Nelson, Chairman, President, and CEO,
National Gypsum Company

"Relationships Are Everything! expresses a fundamental and over-looked truth about business. This book lifts the hood and gives the reader a first-hand look at what really drives a professional practice. If all leaders took to heart the mother-lode of wisdom contained in this book, they and those they lead would be happier and more content, and their practices and their practice groups would be much more successful. This book may evoke some painful self-evaluation, but it will be well worth the experience. After 25 years in private practice and seven years in the corporate world, I only wish I'd had and heeded the insight from this book a long time ago."

Cleat Simmons, Senior Vice President and General Counsel,
SunGard Higher Education

"Common sense reigns. Relationships Are Everything! provides simple, practical steps to improve a professional's ability to build meaningful, lasting relationships. Although much of Mark's approach seems obvi-ous, I constantly found myself wondering, 'If it's so obvious, why don't I do it that way?'"

Mark E. Golman, Partner, Strasburger & Price, LLP

"*Mark's first book,* Rainmaking Made Simple, *was very practical and a great reference guide for our busy attorneys learning to build their practices.* Relationships Are Everything! *complements Mark's first book perfectly and is a very easy read. It is full of practical situations and checklists that our attorneys can incorporate effortlessly into their daily practice. Mark shows you how to make marketing fun while remaining true to your authentic self.*"

Sonia Menon, Director of Professional Recruitment and Development,
Neal, Gerber & Eisenberg LLP

"*There are many books about growing business relationships, but I know of none more pragmatic. From how to meet decision-makers and getting unresponsive partners to market, to inspiring client confidence and securing third-party endorsements, this is a book written from the trenches — 48 chapters of inspired insight applied to the real world. You can read* Relationships Are Everything! *cover to cover or flip through it with your particular issues in mind. It is a work destined to bring positive change to your business development efforts.*"

Patrick J. McKenna, Principal, McKenna Associates Inc., and co-author of
First Among Equals: How to Manage a Group of Professionals

"*At last! A practical guide to helping professionals thrive in an increasingly competitive market. We will be recommending this to all aspiring partners.*"

Giam Swiegers, Chief Executive, Deloitte Australia

"*Mark Maraia has done it again!* Relationships Are Everything! *is the definitive easy-to-implement system for teaching the 'hows and whys' of building lasting business relationships. The wisdom shared in these pages has proven indispensable for me in building one of the fastest growing national franchise companies in the United States.*"

Keith Gerson, President/COO, PuroClean,
The Paramedics of Property Damage

"Relationships Are Everything! *stands in a class of its own as the 'must read' of 2009. If you only have the time to buy, read, and apply the learnings from one book, then make it this one and re-read it every year because the lessons are timeless.*"

Trish Carroll, Director, Galt Advisory

"Relationships Are Everything! *isn't hyperbole. Mark Maraia's newest book captures what I have known for decades — the principles of true friendship building are the keys to a great and rewarding career! As a rainmaker in a global Canadian law firm doing extensive business in the Far East for decades and now in international business along with my legal practice, I have found that Mark's books are perfect if you want hands-on, practical advice packed with anecdotes and checklists. 'Become a better friend and you become a better rainmaker.' This is just one of hundreds of gems you will find in this book that, if applied, will transform your career and convince even the hardened cynics that you can enjoy and excel at business development."*

David I. Matheson, QC, Chairman,
Matheson Global Advisory Group, Toronto

"The breadth of this book is remarkable: from planning to team building to developing unappreciated resources and continued improvement. Mark has once again synthesized what real leaders in the field do best. His book speaks as much to those of us in the corporate world as it does to professionals in private practice."

Fred W. Headon, Avocat principal — Droit du travail, Senior Counsel — Labour and Employment Law, Air Canada

"Mark Maraia is a gifted coach when it comes to relationships and networking for professionals. What sets Maraia apart is his refusal to focus on short-sighted technique; instead, he delivers an overarching theme that drives all aspects of a professional's relationships, and brings true beauty to the practice of law. This book of short, sophisticated vignettes is yet another example of his extraordinary talent, and a must read for the serious professional."

Bobby Guy, Partner, Waller Lansden Dortch & Davis, LLP

"Having the benefit of experiencing the power of effective relationships from the perspective of the salesman in the field through CEO of two publicly traded companies, dean of a graduate school of business, to now serving on the boards of five publicly traded companies, I couldn't be more pleased to read Mark Maraia's useful insight into the how and why of developing personal connections. Regardless of your age or experience, you will find something of use; I highly recommend it."

Peter Browning, former CEO of Sonoco Products Company and a member of five boards of directors, including the board of Nucor Corporation

"Relationships Are Everything! *is a perceptive treatise that should be read by every aspiring attorney and also by partners who are interested in getting more satisfaction out of the law practice while being more successful. Mark Maraia's principles have yielded remarkable results for me, not only in establishing valuable relationships that have lasted for decades, but in handling highly complex cases and difficult situations. The reader will be rewarded by the persistent application of Mark's lessons with respect to focusing business development efforts, identifying the client's needs, being alert to feedback, giving of oneself without expecting a quid pro quo, and enjoying professional activities.*"

Lee A. Freeman, Jr., Partner, Jenner & Block LLP

"*In my role as client relations partner, I found Mark's first book so valuable I bought five extra copies and I lend them out to my partners because of the wisdom found in its pages. One reading is never enough. The same can be said about his second book,* Relationships Are Everything! *It is destined to become the most frequently consulted book on your bookshelf.*"

Milt Stewart, Client Relations Partner, Davis, Wright & Tremaine

"*My formal education and on-the-job experience as a professional engineer and utility executive had led me to seek results largely through technical solutions or business process improvements. Mark's new book,* Relationships Are Everything!, *reinforces what I learned from working with Mark: relationship skills play a critical role in this success equation. I would heartily recommend it to any engineer or business executive who wants to succeed.*"

Steve Schmitt, Vice President-Operations Services, American Water

"*Maraia's second book,* Relationships Are Everything!, *is a clear roadmap for excelling in a tough economy! It's teeming with practical advice you can implement immediately and count on to produce real results. Relationships have never been so critical to success.*"

Mark Thienes, Senior Vice President — Retail, Office Max

"In his latest work, Mark Maraia once again demonstrates his unique ability to cut through the theoretical clutter and present common-sense and proven relationship-building strategies that you can immediately apply to your practice. By providing an easy-to-follow process for applying various skills, he helps you address challenges and barriers to success that you face on a daily basis. The light bulb went on for me throughout the book, and I routinely use a combination of his cross-selling and networking suggestions to forge connections with previously hard-to-access potential clients and referral sources. I have no doubt that this book will become an indispensable reference tool for those professionals truly looking to master the art of networking and build a successful business."

Chuck Keller, Partner, Snell & Wilmer L.L.P.

Relationships Are Everything!

Growing Your Business
One Relationship at a Time

by Mark M. Maraia

Professional
Services
Publishing

ISBN 978-0-9724532-2-6

Published by
Professional Services Publishing
8895 Tappy Toorie Circle
Highlands Ranch, CO 80129
303-791-1042

DEDICATION

To the loving mind in everyone.

TABLE OF CONTENTS

ACKNOWLEDGEMENTS

I once again find myself filled with appreciation and gratitude for the thousands of great clients and co-workers who have inspired much of this work. Since the publication of my first book, *Rainmaking Made Simple*, I've also had the opportunity to engage with many thousands of people who have adopted the principles and techniques it sets forth. These include countless letters and emails from readers who have validated the efficacy of my relationship-based approach to building a practice. I'd love to list them all, but that isn't practical. As anyone who has written a book will tell you, it is truly a collaborative venture. All of the following people made valuable contributions to this work and I thank them from the bottom of my heart:

David Lerner, Cindy Rold, Chris Kirby, Debra Bruce, Greg Teimeier, Chuck Keller, Chris Zinski, David Matheson, Gina Koch, Jennifer Rose, Milt Stewart, Lauren Lynch, Randy Lewis, Debra Snider, and Liz Carver.

I want to pay special thanks to several people who made significant contributions to the book. There were two people who made significant improvements to the Introduction, Cleat Simmons and Debra Snider. Both have a unique talent for editing my words.

Chapter 9 was co-authored by Mark Maraia and Mark Thienes. Chapter 15 was co-authored by Mark Maraia and Elise Schadauer. Chapters 21 and 32 were co-authored by Mark Maraia and John Mitchell. Chapter 29 was initially an article of the same name written by Debra Snider, who has graciously allowed us to include it in this work. Chapter 22 was co-authored by Mark Maraia and Cleat Simmons. In addition,

Cleat, along with my sister, Sue LaFave, improved the readability of all of the chapters of this book. Cindy Rold also made substantial improvements to this book while it was in early manuscript form. I also want to thank Elise Schadauer for helping me organize this book into a readable manuscript form.

Special thanks to Nicola Ruskin for helping me with the book cover and internal art. In addition, thanks once again to Rebecca Taff for the copyediting and book layout.

I've read many books and articles through the years and I've done my best at giving proper attribution. If there are times where I've inadvertently failed to give proper credit, I beg your pardon.

INTRODUCTION

I once worked with a client who was raised in a military family, which greatly influenced how he interacted with people. Not surprisingly, he was very "mission" focused: Tell him the objective of his mission, and he'd do anything to achieve it. But he was so focused on the mission that he ran roughshod over people trying to help him. His firm hired me to help him with something more important than just getting the job done: They wanted him to become more relationship-focused.

During one of our early coaching calls, my client spoke in great detail and with pride about his ability to achieve any mission assigned to him. As I listened to his story, an inspired thought came to me. "The relationship is the mission," I told him. This idea stopped him in his tracks and became his rallying cry during our work together.

And that's the same advice I'm giving the readers of this book. The foundation of your professional practice, no matter the mission, should always be relationships. Focus on building strong relationships, and your business will thrive and prosper. Take relationships for granted or, worse, neglect or abuse them, and you will work much harder to maintain a profit or keep your practice afloat. There is an equally compelling reason for putting relationships first: the inner rewards and psychic compensation.

By their very nature, professionals tend to emphasize their technical expertise and downplay or neglect the human side of their businesses. Perhaps they produce technically superior work, but too often they leave in their wake broken or brittle relationships. There are plenty of technical superstars who don't have a long list of clients — or co-workers — who want to work with them, simply because they don't give relationships the attention they deserve. And in today's market, you can be the Einstein of your field, but still starve if you fail to put relationships first.

I've made it my mission in life to increase relationship literacy within the business world.

Relationships *are* everything because they teach us what we need to learn in the classroom of life. I believe that professionals will improve their businesses if they learn to see the world (and their experiences in it) as a classroom that offers daily lessons. The substance of what is taught in the classroom of life is our relationships, both business and personal. Nevertheless, most of us are reluctant learners. We too often see other people as the problem. If we articulated this reluctance, it might be expressed like this: "If only that person would change, then I'd be happy, or successful, or whatever…." The simple truth is that we often discover our own blind spots, shortcomings, and character flaws through other people, particularly those who push our buttons.

The natural outcome of all this relationship building is a robust network. Rainmakers usually possess a large network and go to great lengths to stay connected to it. But they must still do so one relationship at a time. The network you cultivate over the course of your career is like a fingerprint. It's unique to you and it reflects your character. It's so important that you'll find in this book more than a dozen chapters devoted entirely to how to build and maintain a network.

What if you're behind on building your network? There is an old adage that the best time for planting trees was 20 years ago, and the second-best time is right now. That adage could just as easily apply to networks. If you're behind, there is no better time than now to start building your network. A good place to begin, as you'll learn in Chapter 2, is to start calling on people you truly like and respect — even if they don't hold out a promise of business. Why? Because building a network of people you don't like is drudgery, unsustainable, and not worth doing. Building a network of people you do like is a pleasure well worth undertaking.

ABOUT THIS BOOK

Relationships Are Everything! is an indispensable companion to my first book, *Rainmaking Made Simple*, which provides a framework for the busy professional who wants less theory and more of a desk reference for the skills needed to build a book of business. Similarly, each chapter in *Relationships Are Everything!* is deliberately short, providing a checklist for common situations you'll face every day: meeting with a friend (networking at deeper levels), meeting with a partner or co-worker, releasing negative emotions, delegating dull or routine work, speaking at your firm, and developing the next generation of rainmakers. Furthermore, chapters in the skills section of the book provide an easy-to-follow structure for applying each skill that you can put to work immediately.

Everything in this book comes straight out of the thousands of coaching meetings and phone calls I've had with professionals all over the world, conversations that have given me insight into what works and what doesn't. And the structure still allows plenty of room for spontaneity and customization.

Many professionals believe they must act in unseemly or uncomfortable ways to become rainmakers. I vigorously disagree. You can absolutely remain true to yourself and still be great at selling and marketing. In fact, the truer you remain to yourself, the more effective you'll be as a rainmaker. As I frequently remind my clients, become a better friend and you'll become a better rainmaker. I'll never encourage you to do what's far outside your comfort zone. Instead, I want you to look at everything you do — or fail to do — as something that either strengthens or weakens relationships.

I hope you will consult *Relationships Are Everything!* and *Rainmaking Made Simple* frequently throughout your day to strengthen your relationships and build your practice. May the pages become worn and dog-eared from frequent use!

PART I

Starting
Relationships

Your ability to generate leads
is limited only by your imagination

<table>
<tr><td>1</td></tr>
</table>

FOURTEEN WAYS TO GENERATE LEADS FAST!

WHERE DO I FIND PEOPLE TO HIRE ME?

Many professionals want to know: How do I find people to hire me? It's really not hard. If the thought of generating leads is intimidating, think of it as finding people who need your help. You are surrounded by hundreds of people who can definitely use it. Aside from that, the most obvious and popular way to generate leads is to do great work for clients! However, because this strategy isn't enough to make your practice thrive, here are more lead-generation techniques to think about.

FOURTEEN WAYS TO GENERATE LEADS

1. TOUR A CLIENT'S OR PROSPECT'S BUSINESS OPERATION OR PLANT. This is usually a great way to meet more people in your client's organization. Be alert to opportunities that can only be found during these tours. For example, an employment lawyer can observe whether her client has posted the required notices in accordance with state or federal law. One client of ours did 30 to

40 of these site visits per year, adding a fresh list of names to his contacts list each year.

2. INVITE A HANDFUL OF PEOPLE TO YOUR NEXT PUBLIC SPEAKING ENGAGEMENT. Suppose you'd like to meet dozens of city attorneys but you currently only know two. You can increase that number to 20 or 30 almost overnight if you call dozens of city attorneys before your next presentation — and follow up with them after you've spoken. An Occupational Safety and Health Administration (OSHA) lawyer did something similar with a prospect and picked up an OSHA penalty case from someone he hadn't previously known. These calls won't always generate work like they did for this OSHA lawyer, but they *will* generate leads.

3. LOOK TO YOUR NONPROFIT BOARD CONTACTS. Single out one person per month at each board meeting. Invite the person to have lunch with you so you can learn more about her business. In the span of one year you will generate eleven new leads from your twelve-member board.

4. TAKE A LATERAL PARTNER OR AN AQUAINTANCE FROM YOUR FIRM TO LUNCH. It's easy to keep having lunch with the usual suspects in your firm. The best rainmakers are constantly reaching out to those they don't know well. An easy place to start is with your firm's newest lateral partner or associate. Be sure to invest some time in high-energy conversation with him. One of our clients realized he had lunch with the same six people each month. The real opportunity lies in connecting with 20 other partners in his firm about whom he barely knows.

5. INVITE A TRIED-AND-TRUE REFERRAL SOURCE AND INVITE HIM OR HER TO LUNCH TO SAY "THANK YOU." Saying "thank you" can generate work very quickly. One New York tax lawyer did this with his CPA referral source, which led to another referral at his "thank you" lunch.

6. ASK A PROVEN REFERRAL SOURCE OR FRIEND FOR AN INTRO-DUCTION. Make this request in a meeting other than the one in which you say thanks. Decide before you meet with your referral that you'll ask for an introduction to a person from his net-

work. Simply say, "Do you have any peers at other companies who have expressed some dissatisfaction with their current outside service provider?" Follow up by asking whether he would be comfortable introducing you.

7. IF YOUR GROUP HAS A SPEAKERS' COMMITTEE, SIGN UP TO HELP THE GROUP FIND SPEAKERS. Begin calling people you've always wanted to meet and invite them to speak to your group or to serve on a panel at one of your upcoming meetings. Even if they decline, they'll probably be flattered you asked.

8. CALL ONE DORMANT CLIENT PER WEEK. If you haven't spoken to a dormant client for a while, call to say, "I was thinking about you and wondered how you're doing." Then stop talking and let the person respond! Or close the loop on advice you gave your client. This conveys a sense of caring that is all too scarce in this high-speed world.

9. CLOSE THE LOOP ON ADVICE TO A PARTNER IN YOUR FIRM. This is a variation on number 8 above.

10. INTERVIEW A HANDFUL OF PEOPLE FOR AN ARTICLE.[1] People love to see themselves quoted in print. By writing an article using your contacts you will flatter and show them you respect their ideas and thoughts. It will also add depth, interest, and content to your article. It is also a great way to ensure that the article is actually written!

11. CALL SERVICE PROVIDERS YOU WORKED WITH ON A RECENTLY COMPLETED MATTER. Take them to lunch and ask them how they market their practices. Your fellow service providers can be a great resource for learning better ways to grow your business. Think of them as your board of advisors.

12. ATTEND INDUSTRY CONFERENCES WITH YOUR TOP CLIENTS. More often than not, your clients will introduce you to many new people during the conference.

13. PUT PEOPLE TOGETHER FREQUENTLY. The more you broker someone else's success, the more she will become involved in yours. It also gives you more touches with the market. For

example, you might help a departing contact at an existing client find a senior position in another company.

14. GET YOUR STAFF TO HELP YOU FIND LEADS. Ask them to read the local newspaper through a different set of lenses. One rainmaker had his assistant do this for him every morning. Over the years, she generated tons of leads for her boss and for his partners.

Your local newspaper is a treasure-trove of opportunity. Much to one rainmaker's dismay, his long-time assistant took a new job in another part of the state. At the urging of his coach, this person asked his former assistant if she still wanted to scout out leads for him. She jumped at the chance to track down leads for him again!

There are countless ways to generate leads. If you act on one of these ideas each day, you will soon be generating more leads than you can handle. And don't forget that people need your help, so if you keep that in mind, lead generation will be a positive experience for you.

When trying to choose contacts to call, call those you think will be fun to reach out to.

┌─────┐
│ 2 │
└─────┘

MAKE IT FUN OR YOU WON'T CALL!

Whom Do I Call First?

Every so often we meet clients who are overwhelmed by their full list of contacts and aren't sure whom to call first. If you have lots of names on your contact list, prioritize them according to the categories below, and then call them in order. If you have three people in each category, attempt to reach all three in the first category before going on to the next category.

1. "We're long overdue to get together." These are the people you know well or whose company you really enjoy. Time always flies when you get together with these people. Most rainmakers have many contacts in this category.

2. "I like you." Call people you like, respect, and want to spend more time with. This can be anyone from referral sources to friends or neighbors. There are usually many people in this category for most professionals.

3. "I'd like to spend more time with you." This category includes people you don't know well but you'd like to meet

based on a limited positive knowledge of them. You feel a strong connection to them, even though you haven't spent much time with them.

4. "I CAN LEARN A LOT FROM YOU." Call people who are great networkers or from whom you can learn a great deal. This can include successful business people who have much to teach you.

5. "I CAN TAKE THIS PERSON IN SMALL DOSES." This category includes people you can tolerate but only because they hold great promise of business or leads. The number of people in this category is few, which is a good thing because it's not easy spending time with them.

6. "I DON'T ENJOY THIS PERSON'S COMPANY." People you don't like should be removed from your contact list. You don't have any fun when you call or meet with them, and you dread the idea of spending time with them. In fact, you'd rather go to the dentist for a root canal than meet with these people. If you really can't bear to drop them off your list, hand them off to someone else in your firm who might fit them into one of the five previous categories.

Remember, this is supposed to be *fun*! Don't call or meet with people because someone else thinks they're great prospects. Life is too short and work is too demanding to build relationships you don't enjoy. The simple reality is that you won't stay in regular contact with people you don't like, so stop trying.

Never interpret unreturned messages
as evidence of rejection!

3

EFFECTIVE VOICEMAIL STRATEGIES

WHAT PROTOCOLS DO I FOLLOW WHEN LEAVING MESSAGES?

Two tools have become unavoidable in this communications age: voicemail and e-mail. Sometimes they are misused. Yet, both can be useful allies in your relationship-building efforts. Here are some common-sense protocols to follow so that your messages aren't left unattended by their recipients.

1. MAKE THE TELEPHONE AN ALLY IN YOUR MARKETING EFFORTS. The telephone has been with us for over a century and has helped countless businesses be more effective in selling and marketing. However, the way some professionals resist using the telephone, you'd swear it weighs 1,000 pounds.

I had lunch with a friend not long ago who had started his own consulting business. He had developed an impressive list of prospective clients he wanted to call, containing a mix of people he knew fairly well and some he didn't know at all. However, he was disappointed at the number of calls that were actually getting through. After further discussion, it became obvious that he wasn't trying frequently enough. He realized that he could call each person five times per day, not leave a message, and radically increase his chances of reaching the person in real time, rather than leaving a single voicemail message each week. If you call five times a day and don't reach someone, don't leave a message. Many professionals we coach like the idea of increasing the frequency of their calls without leaving a message but admit it wouldn't have occurred to them.

2. READ NOTHING INTO AN UNRETURNED MESSAGE. The most frustrating thing about selling isn't always the rejection: it's the apparent rejection we interpret from an unreturned phone call. Many professionals see the unreturned phone call itself as evidence of rejection! We frequently remind people that an unreturned phone call is a sign that the person called is busy or has other priorities. Skeptical? Do you return 100 percent of your calls promptly?

3. CALL FREQUENTLY, BUT LEAVE MESSAGES SPARINGLY. Your notes for a single day when trying to contact people who are difficult to reach or whom you really want to reach might look like this:

Called prospect at 8:10 AM. Left message. Called prospect at 8:56 AM. Left no message. Called prospect at 9:40 AM. Left no message. Called prospect at 11:21 AM. Left no message. Called prospect at 1:19 PM. Left no message. Called prospect at 2:45 PM. Left no message. Called prospect at 4:01 PM. Left no message. Called prospect at 6:19 PM. Left no message.

In summary, you made eight calls, but only left one message. The total elapsed time needed for making these eight calls was less than five minutes.

Most professionals have a very short list of prospects they are trying to reach, which makes this strategy even more sensible. If you're only targeting three companies, you might as well do everything you can to improve the odds you'll actually speak to someone. Avoid leaving too many voicemail messages. After a reasonable amount of time has passed, you can leave another message.

If the person you're calling has caller ID, our advice is the same. You can call frequently and if she sees your number pop up and it doesn't result in a message, it shows your thoughtfulness.

ELEMENTS OF AN EFFECTIVE VOICEMAIL MESSAGE

Keep several things in mind when leaving a voicemail message. The world would be a better place if everyone followed these guidelines:

1. ASK A QUESTION. Always leave the recipient with a QUESTION that makes him want to return your call. The right question can act like a seed in the ground. It stays with the recipient well beyond the playback of your message. This requires some thought about what you'll say. For example, your message to a dormant client might be: "Hello, Carol, this is Mark. I was thinking about you and wondered how the deal we worked on together last year turned out. Did it deliver the cash flow you had hoped for? When you have a chance, please call. We're overdue to catch up."

2. USE HUMOR IF POSSIBLE. Humor can make your message memorable. We all need a little more humor in our busy lives. I sometimes leave the following message with the professionals I'm coaching who won't return my calls: "I've left instructions in my will to have my children call you periodically to find out how your meeting with Charlie went."

3. BE SUCCINCT. Leave a message that gets right to the point. Again, in the case where you are calling a dormant client you might say, "I was thinking about you and wondered how you are doing. Please give me a call when you have a moment." Generally speaking, less is more.

4. ADD VALUE. Part of our work with professionals is to help them stay focused and organized. In many cases, leaving a message can trigger an action response. It might contain a question about a specific meeting or phone call we had previously discussed. Even if the person doesn't return the call, more often than not it prompts him to keep the commitment he made to himself.

When to Use E-Mail Instead

We encourage professionals to shift to e-mail after leaving several telephone messages that go unreturned. When *you* get discouraged or the deadline for reaching someone is quickly drawing near, another type of communication such as e-mail could work instead.

It's amazing how promptly some clients will respond to e-mail. Conversely, if you've tried several e-mails without response, perhaps it's time to pick up the telephone.

One consultant participated in a beauty contest and had twice followed up with his contact and left a voicemail message. He was anxious to find out how the prospective client had decided. In these circumstances, sending an e-mail makes a lot of sense.

Persistence Is Key

Your firm's rainmakers have learned from experience that friendly persistence will produce amazing results. Being persistent is always better than doing little or nothing. Giving up may be a mistake, but giving up too early is always a mistake.

Modern communication tools like the telephone, voicemail, and e-mail exist to enhance our ability to connect with others. Used properly, both voice mail and e-mail can provide enormous benefits to your relationship building.

The best rainmakers think of today's non-decision-makers
as a pool of future decision-makers.

4

MEETING MORE DECISION-MAKERS

HOW CAN I BROADEN MY POOL OF FUTURE DECISION-MAKERS?

To some professionals, knowing lots of decision-makers is the holy grail of marketing. They believe knowing more decision-makers will lead to more marketing opportunities. While knowing as many decision-makers as possible can be helpful, all is not lost if you know only a few. Our advice to those worried about not knowing enough decision-makers is to *relax*. A good habit to form is to meet more people. If done correctly, you will meet people who influence the decision-makers and they will rave about you and become your champions.

It's amazing the number of professionals who dismiss taking initiative to contact someone because the person "isn't a decision-maker." All too often, professionals mistakenly treat influencers as if they are invisible. Trash that kind of limited thinking. At the very least, these influencers possess valuable information that can't be gathered anywhere else. Here are five guidelines to keep in mind to broaden your pool of decision-makers.

1. Influencers have valuable information you can't find anywhere else. All of us have met that trusted associate or assistant who is the gatekeeper to someone else. And we may have unintentionally discarded that person or others who have great influence on the actual decision-maker. Influencers have a wealth of information about what the decision-maker thinks and, more importantly, needs.

Building a relationship with an influencer will benefit you in your marketing efforts. Influencers can arm you with information needed to gain access to the decision-maker and they can work with the decision-maker from an informed position. Imagine having access to the powerful executive secretary who can book you a meeting with the decision-maker if he or she likes your message.

2. Find valid reasons for starting a dialogue with decision-makers. If you're an accountant looking for more work within the high-tech world, you must first identify people who orbit that world. Two simple ways to increase the number of decision-makers you are exposed to are (1) to line up a speaking engagement to a high-tech group and start inviting everyone on your wish list to your presentation and (2) to write an article on a timely topic for an industry newsletter or other publication. In less than a week, you can go from knowing two people in that industry to having had a phone conversation with 20 or more.

3. Give your time and attention to others, not solely to decision-makers. All too often, the upward mobility of talented people leads to missed opportunities. You work with Betsy who is not a decision-maker at company A, but she moves to company B, where she becomes a decision-maker. Great rainmakers stay in touch with Betsy to ensure they grow their reservoir of future leaders. Too often, professionals are shocked by a shrinking network because they spent all their time with top people and none with mid-level people.

Junior professionals can't easily build a network of decision-makers because their peers don't yet have enough experience. With time that will change. Many professionals at all levels of seniority dismiss the value of junior executives because they aren't final arbiters on who is hired. That's a mistake. Those junior execs will one day become senior execs. Don't wait until they are elevated to that level before befriending them. If you do, your competitors might already have done so.

4. DECISION-MAKERS ARE CLEVERLY DISGUISED AS ORDINARY PEOPLE ALL AROUND YOU. We all know colleagues who move in-house with a company and people we meet on the other side of a deal. Either could turn into your best referral source.

One professional received a call from a female business owner who handed him a large assignment. Several weeks into the assignment she asked him whether he recalled how they first met. He couldn't remember. She reminded him that she was the secretary for one of his clients a decade earlier! She had gone out on her own to start a very successful business and never forgot how well he had treated her.

5. ALMOST ANYONE CAN BECOME A DECISION-MAKER. Treat everyone with respect because almost anyone could be or could become a decision-maker. It's impossible to predict which non-decision-makers of today will become the decision-makers of tomorrow. For instance, the receptionist and the custodian are two oft-overlooked sources of both information and knowledge. They're often in the know and appreciate being noticed for it. Don't overlook, and in fact do actively cultivate, these sources. Also, while some don't have the authority to hire you, they may have authority to prevent you from being hired. Those who aren't decision-makers will notice when you treat them with respect and it will position you very well down the road when they're elevated to more lofty status.

One lawyer was surprised to learn that the legal assistant, rather than the general counsel, made the outside legal hiring decisions for one company. Title companies have long known that real estate paralegals wield a tremendous amount of hiring influence for their law firms and they go out of their way to court those paralegals. That should be a great lesson to professionals about treating everyone as a potential, if not an actual, decision-maker.

Don't be a fair-weather friend and only make time for people *after* they're promoted to positions of significant responsibility. It shows that you lack class and that you don't treat everyone you meet with the respect they deserve. Generally speaking, the lower someone sits in the hierarchy, the more he or she craves respect.

The best rainmakers and the savviest junior people consider today's non-decision-makers as their pool of future decision-makers. The key is to form as many relationships now with non-decision-makers when you're not pressured to build your own book of business. If you're already feeling the heat, just get started! Your network won't grow by itself, and it will grow faster if it includes more people.

First meetings, like first dates, are far more effective when you go slowly.

5

ACING YOUR FIRST MARKETING MEETING

WHAT QUESTIONS SHOULD I ASK AND WHAT BENCHMARKS SHOULD I ACHIEVE?

If you've never conducted a marketing meeting — or if you have but aren't confident in your marketing skills — it's understandable that you might be nervous about getting it right. Let me put your mind at ease. Your key goal with any first marketing meeting is to develop a great connection with whomever you are meeting. Generally speaking, your motto for almost any first meeting is, "Go slowly."

Relationship building isn't a contest to see how quickly you can secure new work. A minority of rainmakers will insist that you should ask for the business during every meeting, including the very first one. I disagree vehemently. In fact, only one out of every 20 meetings should involve asking for business. You might be thinking, "What do I ask for?" Typically, the only time to ask for work in a first meeting is when you're meeting with someone who came to you as a referral. Where appropriate, you can ask, "What's the next step?" rather than "Can I do your work?"

Whenever you're preparing for a meeting, a threshold question you always want to ask yourself is, "Is this a selling meeting or a networking meeting?" How you prepare for and conduct the meeting will differ depending on your answer to this question. A selling meeting requires a clearly defined next step at the end of the meeting. By contrast, a networking meeting doesn't usually result in a clearly defined next step. In other words, a networking meeting ends more indefinitely. That doesn't mean there isn't a purpose to a networking meeting, but rather the purpose is to establish, or further, a relationship.

FIRST MEETING QUESTIONS

Questions you might ask in any first meeting are simple and will vary depending on your area of expertise. Over time you should be able to develop a target list of four or five questions you know will work very well in your first-time meetings.

Perhaps the worst thing you can do in a first meeting is to go in unprepared and without writing down any questions to ask. Our clients report that having those questions in hand allows them to fill the silence with queries that allow them to gather rich information and display an understanding of, or at least an interest in, the other person's business. As we often advise our clients, the person who asks the most thoughtful, penetrating questions wins the most business.

Ideally, you will have a written list of first meeting questions for three kinds of meetings: selling, networking, and referral. Two questions to *avoid* asking in a first meeting are, "Who does your work?" and "Can we get some of your work?" Nothing will brand you as unprofessional faster.

To make a great impression on someone, ask for feedback on what he likes about his current service providers. If he starts gushing about whomever he currently uses, take copious notes. If he tells you what he doesn't like, it will give you a road map of what it will take to displace them. Consider this free and very valuable market research. You're learning about your competition and your potential customer's needs, likes, and dislikes. It's like being given the answers to the test beforehand, especially if you hope to get business from that person in the future.

FIRST MEETING BENCHMARKS

The best rainmakers often set benchmarks for first meetings to advance a relationship. Here's our list of six benchmarks, including the two most valuable, which are to gain more information and to secure a next step.

1. TALK NO MORE THAN ONE-THIRD OF THE TIME. For extroverts this will be tough. For introverts, it should be easier. However, none of us likes silence. Resist the temptation to fill the silence with your words, unless those words happen to be a thoughtful question.

2. AGREE ON ACTION TO BE TAKEN AT A SPECIFIC POINT IN THE FUTURE. If the first relationship-building meeting is a selling meeting, secure an advance or a definite action that will take place by a specific time. An advance is something you can put on a calendar, even if it's just another meeting or a phone call. But it's scheduled at a specific time.

A networking meeting will require seeking another encounter with the person down the road. Ideally, you should hear people you've met say, "I've enjoyed this. We should do this again" or words to that effect. That is a golden opportunity to call again at a later time to set up another meeting to continue developing the relationship.

3. SET UP A THREE-WAY MEETING. If it's a selling meeting, you might meet with someone else in the prospect's organization. If it's a networking meeting, you might agree to introduce your friend to a potential client or customer. If it's a meeting with a referral, your contact might agree to introduce you to a prospective client.

4. AGREE TO MEET AGAIN IN SEVERAL MONTHS.

5. AGREE TO INTRODUCE YOUR NEW CONTACTS TO SOMEONE ELSE FOR THEIR MUTUAL BENEFIT.

6. PERSUADE YOUR NEW CONTACT TO DIVULGE SOMETHING ON HER WORRY PILE YOU MIGHT BE ABLE TO HELP WITH. If it's a networking meeting and you have persuaded her to share a current need, you'll feel you've established a solid connection. If she

leaves with a smile on her face and makes a genuine reference to "doing this again," you've aced the meeting.

7. Give away advice. Provide information your contact will benefit from because he met with you. It not only enhances his image of you, but he will be favorably disposed to meet with you again.

The most important point to remember about first meetings is to make the connection your primary goal, rather than obtaining work. This takes all the pressure off and tends to make first meetings much more fun. As one of our clients put it, this approach moves first meetings from "abhorrent" to "entertaining." Try it and see for yourself.

Rehearse before any major presentation with a prospective or existing client.

┌─────┐
│ 6 │
└─────┘

PRACTICE MAKES PERFECT IN BEAUTY CONTESTS

How Can Preparation Lead to Winning Contests?

Two clients we coached were asked by their firm to participate in a beauty contest. Although neither was the lead for this particular opportunity, they both served as unofficial leaders of the team. Having been through our coaching program, these two professionals had learned the value of preparation.

Concerned that the proposed team would talk too much during the presentation, they convinced the other eight members on the team to meet for a dry run. Our two clients had learned that the road to winning presentations included preparing everyone on the team for the presentation, practicing it as a team, and getting feedback.[1]

The entire team spent three hours preparing and practicing. Afterward, each team member was better able to grasp his or her role for the presentation. The preparation included doing the presentation, getting feedback from a "mock client," doing another run-through of the presentation, and getting feedback a second time.

At beauty contests most professionals tend to talk too much about themselves and ask too few questions in order to truly understand the prospective client's needs. The two executives we had coached were intent on gathering feedback from the prospective client with the hope the relationship would expand. To meet this goal, the team agreed that no team member was permitted to talk more than two minutes at any one time, and when a team member finished talking, he or she needed to conclude with a question to the client. Sometimes the question was, "Does that answer your question?" Other times it was an invitation for the prospective client to provide more input. The team wanted to have a dialogue, not give a monologue. This later proved to be a key to their success as a team because it coaxed the prospect into talking!

The actual meeting went very well. As one of the team members said afterward, it was one of the best presentations he had ever given as part of a group. And perhaps the best reward for preparing well was receiving a new engagement with the promise of two more engagements from the prospective client. The effort on the front end paid off nicely!

We recommend debriefing as a team after the presentation. Although this team didn't meet after the presentation, they saw the value in debriefing and plan to do a team debriefing after their next presentation.

If you want to enjoy marketing, make the relationship more important than the business that might flow from the relationship.

```
┌─────┐
│  7  │
└─────┘
```

IDEAS TO KICK-START YOUR NETWORKING EFFORTS

WHAT HAVE OTHERS DONE TO START RELATIONSHIPS?

Sometimes it helps to know what works well for others in their efforts to network as you work on improving your own efforts. We hear dozens of success stories from professionals around the globe. If you want to improve your networking efforts, consider what has worked for others — these strategies just might work for you too. Here are four success stories directly related to networking:

1. Act Like a Host

2. Two Calls Are Better Than One

3. When Presenting, Start a Relationship with the Audience

4. Nearly Everyone Is Interesting If You Give Him a Chance

Act Like a Host

A team of four lawyers from the same firm attended a law society meeting in Singapore. This meeting was one of those functions for which there was no official host. These lawyers took to heart the notion of "acting like a host rather than a guest" by positioning themselves at the entrance to the meeting hall. They proceeded to greet every person who walked into that meeting and met everyone who came to the function, including many in-house lawyers.

Not only did they enjoy themselves and meet loads of prospective clients, but those attending felt welcomed by the unofficial hosts of the event. The number of events that could be unofficially hosted in this way is virtually endless.

Two Calls Are Better Than One

A consultant, we'll call him Al, had let a number of his contacts wither due to the pressures of his practice. One of these contacts had been an associate in years past but had moved on to another position. The relationship was strong enough that Al attended his buddy's wedding a decade ago. However, it had been two years since their last contact. Al wanted to reconnect, but wasn't sure how. He felt it would be too strange to suggest meeting for lunch after a two-year hiatus.

His coach suggested making two or three calls over several months before suggesting a meeting for lunch as a means of easing back into the relationship, which was far more comfortable for him. So he called the first time just to reconnect, and it wasn't until his second call that he suggested they meet for lunch.

When Presenting, Start a Relationship with the Audience

A litigator in the Midwest asked his coach for ideas on how to deliver a preventative litigation seminar to senior executives. His coach reminded him that the goal of speaking is to start a relationship with members of the audience. This lawyer realized that he didn't have a well-developed network of senior executives and wanted to use his speaking to grow this aspect of his network.

That is exactly what he did. He began doing presentations locally and in other parts of the United States. Before long, he landed two new clients because of a presentation he delivered in Phoenix, Arizona. What surprised him was how effective his speaking was at generating new work for his partners. More impressively, he had met another 200 business executives who otherwise wouldn't have known he existed.

Nearly Everyone Is Interesting If You Give Him a Chance

One of our Canadian clients used some of our common sense approaches to networking during a dinner party with his wife's friends that helped him enjoy an evening that he was dreading. At previous dinner parties with this group, the participants typically talked about uninteresting and perfunctory topics that left him ready to leave within minutes of arriving. This time, he resolved to approach it differently. On the way to the dinner, he enlisted the support of his wife in asking questions that he'd learned in our coaching workshop. The goal was to ask thoughtful questions that would invoke more energy and excitement into the conversation.

For example, they asked: "What is your greatest fear?" and "What is your greatest accomplishment?" The questions were serious, yet provoked interesting discussions, and in some cases great debates, in which everyone became involved. This couple spent their time thinking of great ways to keep others talking and they thoroughly enjoyed themselves. For the first time, this professional wanted to spend his time listening instead of being the center of attention. What he discovered is that these "boring people" were actually quite interesting.

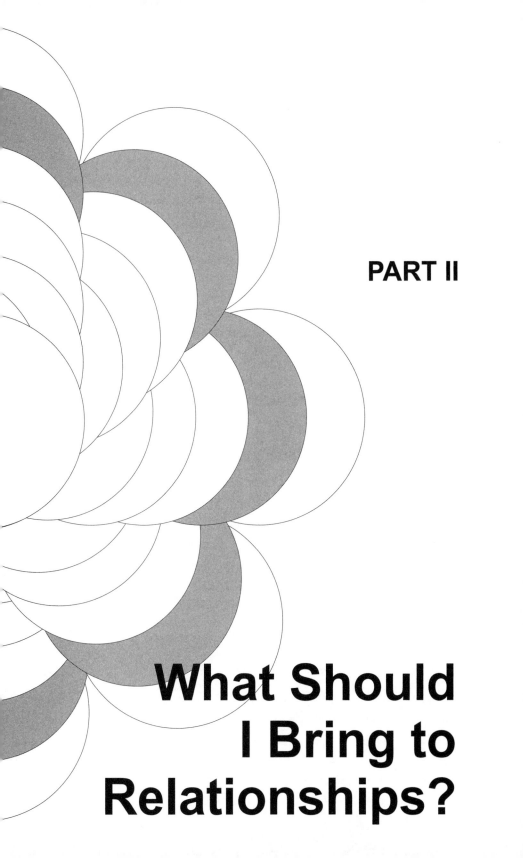

PART II

What Should
I Bring to
Relationships?

*If your cup is always running over, you don't mind sharing
what's in your cup.*

8

MARKETING WITH AN ABUNDANCE MENTALITY

Can Helping Others Improve My Marketing Efforts?

The finest rainmakers in professional services have always impressed me with their boundless generosity. Most rainmakers operate from an abundance mentality, and your marketing efforts will pay huge dividends if you do the same.

A more common belief from which many people operate is scarcity thinking. To present the scarcity mindset as a metaphor, imagine a person sitting by a fireplace refusing to put wood into the fireplace but still expecting heat from the fire. It's obvious there will be no fire without wood. It should be equally obvious that you'll have very little marketing success when your primary concern is helping yourself. That's exactly how limited thinkers approach marketing. If you help as many people as you can in as many ways as you can, you'll be giving your marketing plenty of fuel.

SCARCITY THINKING TO AVOID

"I'll take anything that walks through the door." When you're really good at selling and networking, you can afford to be very choosy and not take just anything that walks in the door. If you are desperate for more work, all you communicate is your desperation.

"I don't want to do people favors (put people together) because they might take advantage (or it's a waste) of my time." If you don't invest time to help others, they are far less likely to help you.

"I need to get work from this prospect today because my workload is down." This kind of thinking makes us ineffective at relationship building. We are better served to let the relationship unfold at a natural pace.

I'm sure at one time or another we've all had these kinds of thoughts. It's okay to have them on rare occasions, but don't let them dominate your thinking and behavior.

If some clients don't fit with the firm's strategy, refer them to some friendly competitors. It may sound ridiculous, but it can be a win/win for all.

GROWING INTO AN ABUNDANCE MENTALITY

The great inventor Buckminster Fuller is a wonderful example of someone who grew into an abundance mentality. He didn't always think that way. On the very day he contemplated suicide he awoke to the awareness that he would dedicate the rest of his life to the service of mankind. He went on to develop nearly 500 patents. Instead of keeping the sales proceeds from his inventions for himself, he donated all the profits from those patents to charity. At the end of every month, he gave away every dime he earned from his inventions and never wanted for anything. Talk about trusting that he would be provided for!

When you sell from abundance, you genuinely try to help someone, even if that means the person is better served by *not* hiring you. Should you find yourself in this situation, the more often you can say, "I can't help you," "You don't need me, you need an accountant," or "Sam at another firm is the best person to help you," the more your credibility skyrockets. It may seem like suicide to do that, but you will find *nothing* else you do builds trust faster.

PUTTING ABUNDANCE MENTALITY INTO PRACTICE

Try this mental exercise to put abundance into practice. Before your next meeting, adopt the mindset that you are offering a thousand-dollar bill to your friend, client, or contact. Not literally, of course, but I'd like you to approach every meeting with this mindset. (For those readers who might be thinking, "I don't have anything that valuable to offer," beware. That is scarcity thinking, too.) If you consciously attempt to give away a thousand dollars' worth of ideas every time you meet with someone, that person will *always* want to meet with you.

Don't get hung up on the economics of this suggestion. Focus on the feeling you get from doing this. Here's one of our client's reactions to putting abundance thinking into practice: "The meeting went better than I could possibly have envisioned! Tom is extremely interested in the potential venture, and if his company invests to the number that was discussed, my contact is 40 percent to his goal with one person. In addition, if Tom's company invests, he brings a whole new set of potential investors. My contact walked out of there on Cloud Nine and was extremely appreciative of the meeting. I walked out of the meeting feeling really good that I had helped two people take a step closer to their respective goals. I really don't think that getting business from either of them could be as rewarding as that feeling!"

Both networking and selling are much easier and more enjoyable when approached from abundance. As this client found out, putting people together ended up being a welcome break from his practice. Selling from abundance will require you to examine your core beliefs. You might not like all that you uncover. It might even take some real soul-searching. But the fruits of that effort will be worth it. In the final analysis, marketing from abundance is an extraordinary act of faith and I *know* you can do it. We all have the capacity for it. What we need to develop is the willingness to operate from it.

Make the choice for greatness at something today.

9

IN PURSUIT OF GREATNESS

How Can I Make Greatness My Objective?

At some point in my adult life, I wondered why I leapt out of bed most mornings and charged off to tackle the world. Then the answer came to me: I love coaching others to greatness in their relationships! Some might call it my passion, because passion and greatness go hand-in-hand. You might also call it the daily pursuit of excellence, both in myself and in those I serve. There is meaning and purpose in striving for greatness. When your calling and greatness intersect, you've embarked on a sacred undertaking. Greatness that doesn't serve a higher purpose is unsatisfying and, in the end, meaningless.

What Is Greatness?

So what is greatness? I see it simply as being the best at something — noticeably better than nearly everyone else. We were each put on this planet for some unique purpose. The beauty of greatness is that it is truly everywhere and can be achieved by everyone. The sad thing is that most never achieve it, mistakenly thinking it is out of reach, a fantasy, not a feasible reality.

Many, perhaps most of us, spend our lifetimes miscast in a self-created role that postpones or possibly forever prevents our appointment with greatness. At some point, many allow mediocrity to become their fate and settle for far less than they could be. But it need not be that way. There is potential for greatness in all of us whether we're 22 or 72. Cast in the correct role, each person can find it, polish it, and let it shine!

HAVE YOU MADE GREATNESS YOUR OBJECTIVE?

The first question you must answer is, "Have you made greatness your objective?" Greatness can be a level you seek to achieve at work, in your personal life, in your spiritual life, or in your physical condition. The active pursuit of greatness and the passion that comes with it are certainly prerequisites for greatness. As you move along the path to greatness, you realize that it's the journey, not the destination, that brings joy. You can continue to raise your "personal bar" of performance to higher and higher levels. There will be bumps in the road, as with any journey. Indeed those bumps serve to test your resolve and lift you to higher levels of achievement. Anticipate the bumps and the setbacks, but never lose sight of your objective — greatness.

My great fortune came in 1990 when, as a good lawyer, I decided to leave the profession to pursue becoming a great coach. I risked everything to strive for my passion — coaching others to greatness in their relationships. Each year I re-evaluate my mission, set the bar even higher, redefine what greatness means to me, and set out for new heights.

Could I have become a *great* lawyer? Maybe. Fortunately for my clients, I chose instead pursuit of excellence as a coach. So let me ask you a question. Do you want to be great? If so, at what? We are *all* called to greatness, but few choose to listen to the call. Greatness is calling you each and every day. Will you hear the call today?

Your champions will be more effective when they ask rather than tell.

10

COACHING INTERNAL CHAMPIONS

WHAT CAN I OFFER MY CHAMPIONS TO ENSURE I AM HIRED?

M any rainmakers and neophytes alike are fooled into thinking that they'll be hired in short order if they cultivate a strong advocate or champion within the company they are courting. That isn't always the case. One professional learned via his champion within a company that the incumbent service provider had over-billed this client. Given that fact, this professional erroneously assumed that being hired was inevitable. He was wrong. It turns out that he never established his champion's commitment to hiring him.

WHAT IS A CHAMPION?

A champion is someone in a prospective client organization who wants to hire you even if no one else in the organization knows you exist. Think of this person as an advocate for hiring you over all the other available choices in the marketplace. However, developing a champion within a client organization doesn't mean you'll be hired. More often than not, it means you'll have to go through a two-pronged process to be hired. First you must assess how much of an advocate your champion is, and then you'll need to help him or her make *your* case in front of peers or superiors.

There are "champions," and then there are *champions*. There is a striking difference between a champion who'll put his credibility on the line to hire you and one who'd mildly prefer you to his current counsel. Your chance of success will vary accordingly. If your contact really isn't solidly convinced that you're the best person for the job, he won't be very convincing with his internal audience. And he certainly won't risk political capital to bring you in.

If your champion is a zealous advocate for you or very unhappy with his existing service provider, he'll go much farther out on a limb. He might even gather facts and data to support your hiring or to show how poorly his current provider is doing. What may come as a surprise to you is that so many inside champions are naive about the decision-making process within their own organizations.

Contrast the "champion" who forwards an e-mail with your background materials to Cecelia in his organization versus another "CHAMPION" who calls Cecelia directly to explore her satisfaction with her current employment counsel and actively seeks to secure a three-way meeting with the three of you.

It doesn't take a genius to figure out that your odds in the latter scenario are far better than in the former.

A CHAMPION'S DEGREE OF CREDIBILITY

Always assess how much credibility your champion possesses. If her opinion carries lots of weight, that will work in your favor. If she is new, she may not have much credibility with others in her organization. If your champion lacks much internal credibility with the audience she is trying to persuade, the manner in which she approaches the sale will often spell the difference between success and failure.

Regardless of your champion's credibility, usually she'll be more effective when using an *ask* rather than *tell* approach with others in the organization. The best way to test out how a champion will approach the internal sale is to ask how he or she intends to approach the meeting with the committee or person making the hiring decision. If she says things like, "I will tell [or argue or insist] that you are far better and more cost-effective," you might have an ineffective champion. This is *telegraphing* the intention to tell, not ask.

HELPING A CHAMPION MAKE *YOUR* CASE

Even though your champion might be unhappy with the outside provider he's using, he might not be able to do anything about it because someone else makes all hiring decisions. If that's true, you will need to coach your champion on how to persuade the decision-maker to give you a try.

In a very real sense, you have to equip your champion to ensure you're hired. The process he faces is strikingly similar to the one you would go through if you were talking to the decision-maker directly. Think about the questions you would want to have answered if you were the decision-maker, brainstorm a list of questions to be used by your champion, and be sure he buys into using them. Sometimes winning over the champion is the easy part. Helping the champion win over his boss or a crucial committee can be very hard work.

A large number of professionals are naturally adept at cultivating champions. I've seen many rainmakers get tripped up because they didn't understand how to help their champions make the sale internally. It's the rare person who can convert those champions into paid work almost every time. I hope this chapter has given you some ideas on how to do exactly that.

Curiosity isn't billable right away, but it will generate huge rewards in the long run.

11

RE-IGNITE YOUR CURIOSITY

HOW CAN CURIOSITY HELP ME IMPROVE MY RELATIONSHIPS?

When we coach professionals, we're often asked what sets great rainmakers apart from the pack. We've found that successful rainmakers usually have a tremendous amount of curiosity. Their curiosity leads them into relationships and opportunities that generally pay huge rewards over time.

Great rainmakers are innately curious. We all know people who, when we meet them, have a way of putting us at ease. We may even walk away from a conversation with them and realize we don't know much about them. What sets them apart? They enjoy learning from others and they're always asking questions and wondering about things. This attitude, or way of thinking, is genuine and is also a powerful advantage in building deeper relationships.

Litigators are especially curious as they prepare for court — digging and looking for facts to win their cases. They are thoroughly prepared once in the courtroom, where a good strategy is to "never ask a question you don't know the answer to." It is the rare litigator who is able to break from this formula of "having the answers" outside the courtroom. We'd see a lot more lawyers who are rainmakers if they could change their formulas.

Human beings are all born curious. When we work with clients, we ask them whether they find people naturally interesting. Many haven't even thought about it. Unfortunately, curiosity gets suppressed as we grow up — the school system beats it out of us and our jobs finish it off. We are bombarded by barriers that keep us from being curious: lack of time, value on billable work, or the desire to have the answers. Eventually we lose interest in learning.

CURIOSITY REAPS REWARDS

Imagine the return on curiosity if you were to re-ignite yours: new information and improved relationships that could reinvigorate your practice. Although curiosity isn't billable, it will help you generate billable work six months or a year into the future.

One of our clients found herself in a situation with a client who was a former real estate broker and a "tough nut to crack." She didn't expect him to open up, but when she asked a high-energy question about his assistant — someone who has been with him for 15 years and has moved from company to company with him — she learned about his full career history. One curious question can strike a chord with another person, allowing the person to open up. In the process the relationship is improved and you know more than you did before.

Curiosity is also one of our best assets, taking us down unexpected and exciting paths. One of our clients expressed his childhood dream of getting his pilot's license. When he was probed about this, his passion was obvious. By our next session, he had re-ignited his curiosity, found a flight school training program, taken the training, and received his pilot's license in record time. In addition, following through on his curiosity reinvigorated his practice and his passion for his work. Rather than suppressing his curiosity, this individual took an unexpected yet rewarding path. And he's so glad he did.

One caveat worth mentioning: Try to avoid using your curiosity for self-serving ends. Recently a lawyer friend of mine was lamenting the outcome from a situation many law firms find themselves in. She was at an event at which two lawyers had the opportunity to talk with a client guest. Lawyer A had known the client for some time and focused on asking him about "deals." Lawyer B, a former in-house attorney himself, was meeting the client for the first time. He asked about the client's business, how he handled specific situations, and what kept him up at night. Consequently, the client became very engaged in the conversation with Lawyer B. After the event, it was evident that adding Lawyer B to the service team for the client would be beneficial. Lawyer A refused to do this and actually slowed the relationship-building process with this client. As is evident from this example, when curiosity stems from "being of service" it is genuine and engaging.

BE INTENTIONAL WITH YOUR CURIOSITY

Many times professionals tell us they can't or aren't comfortable asking questions of their friends or clients because they'll be perceived as selling something. But asking questions, especially thoughtful high-energy questions about another person's work, life, or hobbies, shows you are interested. When you're curious about another person, your high-energy questions and feedback questions will bubble up naturally.

Stifling our natural curiosity actually takes more energy than expressing it. You will find that when you are intentional with your curiosity you'll choose high-energy questions that serve you well. The responses are bound to be interesting and enjoyable, even more fun. And when it's fun, you'll follow your curiosity more often. You'll surely reinvigorate your practice. You may even become reinvigorated about life.

Curiosity doesn't cost a dime and can be implemented right away. What's holding you back from your curiosity? What would you like to know about a client but were too preoccupied to ask? Try re-igniting your curiosity today. Plan your high-energy question and get back on track to reinvigorating your practice.

The more true you remain to yourself, the more effective your marketing.

┌─────┐
│ 12 │
└─────┘

REMAINING TRUE TO YOURSELF

How Can Authenticity Improve My Marketing?

Significant numbers of professionals hate marketing and tend to think of it as acting totally contrary to their natural personalities and values. Unfortunately, there is a pervasive belief that maintains you can't market your practice *and* remain true to yourself. That couldn't be further from the truth. In fact, the most effective way to build your practice is to rigorously maintain your integrity. It is axiomatic that we are usually best at what we enjoy or are passionate about, and will tend to do those things we most enjoy. So make what you enjoy part of building your practice.

If you dread the thought of going to conferences or trade shows, don't make going to these venues the centerpiece of your marketing efforts. On the flip side, if you love conferences or trade shows, make it a point to attend two to three per year. Make those things that involve your unique passions an integral part of your efforts. I know of one rainmaker who parlayed passion for wine into some of his most effective business development. In another case, a rainmaker developed a killer network through the years because of an annual fishing and camping trip that he was invited to. Still another professional is a gourmet cook who hosts memorable dinner parties with intimate groups of prospects and referral sources. A well-respected accountant in a large city in Florida loved to travel to England, so he started arranging tours to England for other accountants. It is not coincidental that the tours he headed also led to increased business in his practice.

It also helps to involve others who are significant to you in building your practice. Some professionals consider their spouses the most valuable part of their networks because they are great supporters and champions. And, obviously, if you enjoy activities with your spouse, that will also help build your practice and, in the end, everyone benefits. The key is to reflect on what you're good at and go do it!

*Double your fun and you're more likely to
double your revenues.*

13

FUN CAN DRIVE YOUR MARKETING EFFORTS

AM I HAVING ENOUGH FUN WITH MY MARKETING?

Our coaches presume that it's not possible to have too much fun when you're developing your practice. It doesn't matter whether your book of business is $20,000 or $20 million. If you focus too early and too heavily on results and ignore fun or enjoyment, you will *slow down* your progress toward your goals! The importance of having fun can't be overstated. The larger someone's book of business, the more this message resonates. Not only should the process you follow involve plenty of fun, but the end-result you seek (i.e., the work and/or the people you work for) should also be fun or enjoyable.

Although it's not obvious, this approach is far more pragmatic than idealistic. One professional was lamenting his lack of progress in marketing a new area of his practice. Moments earlier he'd shared that he had taken one of those personality tests that characterized him as a dolphin. When asked what that meant, he said, "Dolphins like to have fun." Almost comically he then proceeded to emphasize his need for "greater self-discipline" to develop this new area of his practice. Upon being reminded of his need to have fun and that his chances of achieving greater success through self-discipline were nil, the smile on his face was priceless. Trying to increase your book of business through self-discipline will work for some people, but not this guy, and he's not as unusual as you might think. Many more people would double their books of business if they focused on fun, compared with those people who will double their books of business through greater self-discipline.

Our coaching method has always emphasized fun and enjoyment as an important factor in effective marketing. We're just getting more adamant and strident about its importance. For example, our ideal client isn't someone who wants to double a healthy seven-figure practice — it's someone who wants to double or triple the amount of enjoyment he or she is having in an existing seven-figure practice. What's really fun for us is when a client starts out doubtful that she can double her fun and several months later reports that she achieved what she thought was impossible.

Our coaches frequently ask clients some variation of this question: "Are you having more fun today than you were two months ago?" If the answer is no, it takes our dialogue in a much more spirited direction. If the answer is yes, our coaches believe they're serving a valuable function. We've worked with some great clients through the years. In one case, a former client, who happened to be working with another business development coach provided by her new firm, admitted that if she'd had the choice she would have hired a Maraia & Associates, Inc., coach again. Her new firm was providing the coach at no cost to her, and it was clear she was getting value from the coaching. But she wasn't gushing about the experience. When she was asked whether the coach had inquired about what kind of work she found most fun to pursue, her energy level spiked. She replied that he had not, but that question really resonated with her. Her increased enthusiasm was palpable for the remainder of the conversation.

You might be thinking, "I've been working too hard to even consider what might be fun." If that describes you, try this exercise. Go through your contacts list and choose three people you feel would be fun to call. That is the *only* criterion you want to keep in mind as you go through the list; there is no profit motive needed here. Notice your energy for picking up the phone to call someone. If your energy level for calling isn't at least 9 on a 10-point scale, keep searching through your list. Once you find three people who would be fun to call, be sure to follow through and call them. You'll be well on your way to letting fun drive your marketing.

There are other ways to increase the fun factor. Consider removing the anchors holding you back from fun. Firing your worst client (or highest maintenance client) can send the fun quotient immediately higher. As we sometimes have to advise clients: "If it's torture, stop doing it!" If you hate public speaking, stop using that as your vehicle for building your practice. Play to your strengths rather than investing energy in shoring up your weaknesses. This doesn't mean you should ignore your weaknesses; just don't put lots of energy into them. One unit of energy applied to a strength will deliver a greater return than one unit of energy expended in shoring up a weakness.

In the final analysis, fun matters, and it's far more likely to deliver *results*. The paradox is that those results will come more readily as a by-product of making fun your goal.

The person who can release negative emotions is profoundly more peaceful and effective than the person who can't or doesn't know how.

14

RELEASING NEGATIVE EMOTIONS

How Can I Keep Negative Emotions from Ruining Relationships?

This chapter covers a topic about which almost everyone knows very little — releasing negative emotions. In our coaching work, we frequently find clients who are stuck or hijacked by negative emotions or feelings. The person who is able to release these negative emotions is profoundly more peaceful, happier, and more effective compared to the vast majority of people who can't or don't know how to release negative emotions.

LETTING GO OF NEGATIVE EMOTION IS A POWERFUL TOOL

Like most of us, you've probably been in situations that leave you with negative emotions — the back-stabbing or self-centered partner who upset you again, the client who makes ridiculous demands, and the staffer who won't do what you ask — these are just a few examples.

With the powerful tool we advocate, you'll be able to actually feel and identify a negative emotion and let it go entirely. Most of us want to control or manage that type of emotion because it leaves us with a lingering, negative feeling and additional stress.

Anyone can use this tool to deal with negative emotions in the moment and later if the negative feeling resurfaces. We've all experienced replaying a negative experience over and over in our minds. Rejecting the negative emotion actually interrupts this doom loop. Rejecting negative emotions can be used in an infinite number of situations, both personal and business, without anyone ever knowing you are doing it.

THE THOUGHT PROCESS

The tool we suggest is a thought you say to yourself. The next time you notice you've become overcome with negative emotions or are getting into a lather about something, ask yourself: "What am I feeling at this moment?"

Once you are fully in touch with the feeling or emotion, make a silent declaration to yourself that you *don't want it* anymore. For example, suppose you're extremely angry with the idiot who cuts in front of you on the highway and nearly gets you both killed. Your thought might be, "I do *not* want this anger [or if felt more intensely, rage]."

Then replace the feeling with a constructive thought or the conscious choice to have a positive state of mind. Your thought when fully expressed might be something like, "I do *not* want this anger. I choose to be at peace instead."

It's crucial to realize that when you first start using this thought process, it may feel awkward. Like any new skill, it requires practice. Over time, it will become a habit and you'll find yourself working through situations in minutes rather than obsessing about them for days, weeks, and months! When you're new to using this thought process, you won't always feel a palpable sense of relief. Your first internal utterance of this statement may leave you just as angry or enraged as before. In that case, repeat it over and over again. When you stay with it, you'll eventually begin to feel an obvious sense of relief.

When I am into ruthlessly judging someone, it takes many repetitions before I feel a palpable sense of relief. And when I'm heavily invested in being right, it might take months and thousands of repetitions before it finally brings me relief. The key is that it works for me 100 percent of the time and it can work for you too!

CHOOSING PEACE

I've asked hundreds of people whether they have a process for dealing with negative emotions, in the moment, and very few of them do. If you don't have a process, try the tool we introduced above right now before you finish reading this chapter. Search your mind for a negative emotion that has you in its grip and start practicing!

Once you begin to practice this thought process, you'll notice that fewer things bother you. You'll also notice that when you are bothered by something, the negative emotion doesn't hijack you for quite as long as it would have before. It tends to work best for people who've grown sick and tired of recurring negative emotions — people who conclude: "There must be a better way."

Imagine not just dealing with negative emotions, but releasing them entirely. That may sound too good to be true. But it is straightforward, it's simple, and it works. If you do try it, please write me and let me know how it worked. After over 20 years of practicing this thought process, I've concluded that peace is most definitely something we can choose!

Don't let urgency overcome your priorities; rather live *your priorities. Learn to stay connected to what's really important to you.*

┌─────┐
│ 15 │
└─────┘

WHEN SERVICE FALTERS

CAN BURNOUT HURT SERVICE AND HOW DO I RECOVER FROM IT?

Have you ever found yourself in any of these situations? A client keeps calling, usually with a complaint; the number of fires you're putting out seem to be increasing; you never have time to go to lunch; you don't remember the last time your family took a vacation; your wife is bugging you to spend more time with the kids. Been there, right? Most likely you have been, or are currently in, the throngs of burnout.

Burnout is a serious problem among professionals in stressful jobs, especially lawyers. It can affect you whether you're a law student, a new lawyer, or a veteran lawyer. Demanding schedules, billable-hour expectations, client needs, lack of balance between professional and personal lives — all can lead to burnout.

Ignoring burnout could result in serious physical and emotional outcomes such as physical illness, a nervous breakdown, depression, substance abuse, marital discord — even dropping out of the profession.

RECOGNIZING BURNOUT

You might think burnout sneaks up on you. But you probably already know it's approaching. Those internal conversations you have with yourself are warning you. If you're able to recognize its symptoms, you have a greater chance of turning it around and keeping it at bay. Looking forward to a future event more than enjoying what's right in front of you is a common symptom of burnout. Here are other symptoms of burnout to be aware of:

1. YOU HAVE MORE UNHAPPY OR FRUSTRATED CLIENTS TODAY THAN YOU DID SIX MONTHS AGO. This is a huge red flag because it signals a service failure. You can't stay ahead of things and you spend your time reacting to fires. In coaching a variety of business people, we've found the professional who finds herself here has trouble saying no.

2. YOU ARE ALWAYS AVAILABLE. You never turn off your BlackBerry®; you are reachable all the time.

3. A DISPROPORTIONATE NUMBER OF YOUR STAFF ARE FRUSTRATED. They grumble and might even be poorly performing their work.

4. YOU HAVE NOT TAKEN A VACATION IN THE LAST SIX MONTHS TO A YEAR.

5. YOU TAKE A VACATION, BUT YOU WORK. You don't unplug your BlackBerry or your laptop; you might even call the office.

6. YOU'RE OVERSCHEDULED.

7. URGENCY OVERCOMES PRIORITIES. You no longer do what is most important to you.

8. YOUR FAMILY OR SIGNIFICANT OTHER BEGS YOU TO SPEND TIME WITH HIM OR HER.

How to Turn Burnout Around

While many of the professionals we coach recognize the burnout they feel, few really know how to turn burnout around. Some want to push through it. But if you keep pushing yourself, the burnout will only get worse. To turn around burnout, it's essential to reconnect to what's important to you. Here are some suggestions:

1. START SAYING NO MORE OFTEN. You might love the opportunities and challenges coming your way, but repeatedly saying yes can lead to burnout. We've found that professionals who have trouble saying no also lack confidence in their selling skills. They operate from a place of scarcity, not believing there'll be future opportunities if they turn down work.

2. START DELEGATING WORK TO OTHERS. Is there really a good reason to do all of the work yourself? If the right people have been hired, you can delegate client, administrative, and business development work to your assistant or associates. It can be helpful to put a process in place as work comes in so that you and your assistant know who's responsible for what.

3. SCHEDULE A VACATION. One of our coaches was working with an associate who kept putting off her vacation because a closing date kept changing. She felt she would never have a chance to take a vacation. The coach suggested she stop letting the schedule control when she would go on vacation. When the associate realized her schedule was controlling her life and causing her to feel burnout, she scheduled her vacation and let her colleagues know about it. By reconnecting with her need to take time off, this associate was able to take that vacation and return to her practice with renewed energy. And her colleagues were fully capable of handling the closing on their own.

4. WHEN YOU SCHEDULE A VACATION, SCHEDULE A WEEK. Taking one day off is not enough time to relax and re-energize. Take enough time off to *fully* relax. If you're incredibly busy before and after a vacation, you may need to delegate better, learn to say "no" more often, and let go of some control. You may even want to learn *how* to take a vacation by taking more vacations.

5. DEFINE PARAMETERS WHEN ON VACATION. It is possible to stay connected to the office without letting it control or distract from your vacation. Set parameters. Try this: Check your e-mail and voicemail once a day. You could also have your assistant check your messages and notify you if needed. Realistically, only a small percent of the time someone will need you or your input while you're on vacation. Either of these suggestions lets you stay ahead of messages.

6. SCHEDULE "WHITE SPACE" DURING YOUR DAY OR WEEK. White space is unscheduled time set aside to handle unknowns. When you run from pillar to post you rarely have time to deal with the unexpected. But if you schedule white space you give yourself a buffer to handle those unknowns.

7. TURN OFF YOUR BLACKBERRY. You don't have to be connected ALL OF THE TIME. Turning off your PDA or BlackBerry will give you a break from the constant temptation to read and respond to the messages.

8. LIVE YOUR PRIORITIES. Honor your inner prompt that says, "I'm not having fun." Avoid losing your sanity, your health, or your family. Connect to what's important in your life and work to stay there.

Do you recognize any of the symptoms of burnout for yourself, right now? If you're facing burnout, try one or two of the suggestions for turning burnout around today. Schedule a vacation. Delegate two or more things from your plate to someone else. Just say no!

Turning around burnout — and ultimately, avoiding it — is within your control. You will feel better and your clients, staff, and family will thank you for living your priorities!

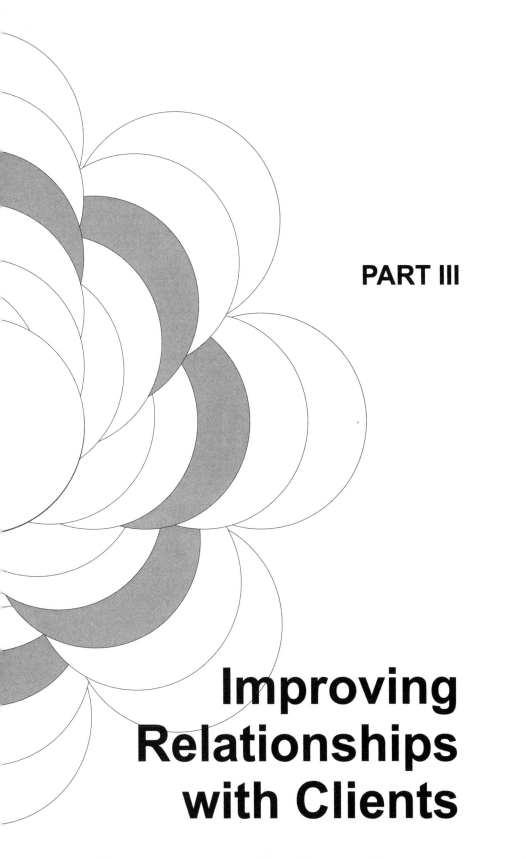

PART III

Improving Relationships with Clients

Be intentional about the kind of
networking you do.

16

THE THREE LEVELS OF NETWORKING

COULD I IMPROVE MY MARKETING BY GIVING MORE TO OTHERS?

In our work as coaches, we find it crucial to assess our clients' attitudes toward networking. Everyone we work with comes to us with different attitudes about networking. We see those attitudes falling into one of three categories or levels.

At Level 1, the attitude is "Take, take, take." Many of our clients have grown to hate the very word "networking" because of their exposure to Level 1 networkers. All of us have been on the receiving end of a Level 1 networker. Such a networker is easy to recognize. He talks non-stop about himself and what he's looking for with little or no concern about helping you. Meanwhile, you're thinking to yourself, "I'm never meeting with this idiot again!" One of our clients was on the receiving end of a person like this recently, and it served as a valuable learning experience for her. It drove home how poorly she'd come across to another if she did the same thing. She also had no interest in continuing a relationship with this person.

At the next level, what we will call Level 2, the networker is more interested in bargaining or "giving to get." This level has a sense of fairness to it. It feels fair to give *this* in return for getting *that*. Many professionals have built a solid book of business by networking with this attitude. The vast majority of people (80 to 90 percent) approach networking and relationships in this way.

There is nothing inherently bad about Level 2 networking. Throughout the business world, there are a dizzying number of consultants and coaching organizations teaching this form of networking. *Forbes* magazine has even devoted an entire issue to it.[1]

The Level 2 networker approaches networking with an attitude of scarcity; it becomes almost instinctual to focus on what's needed to acquire new business, and what it will cost in the bargain. A statement you might hear from such a networker is, "I don't want to ask this person for a favor and use up my precious capital." You can become a rainmaker with a healthy book of business with this attitude, but it will be a long and arduous process.

If you really want to stand out, take your networking to Level 3, the level we ask our clients to adopt. Many who try it become reinvigorated about networking. Level 3 networkers approach networking, and life in general, with an attitude of abundance. Their actions are driven by a genuine desire to give to or help others. They approach networking in this way because they derive enjoyment from the activity itself — giving is the reward. Abraham Lincoln called this kind of giving the "better angels of our nature."[2]

What is wonderful and powerful about Level 3 networking is the depth of relationships that can be developed. You can actually improve your relationships exponentially when your wealth spring never runs dry.

The good news is that you won't have much competition in this rarified air. The bad news is that you will encounter many people at Level 1 and Level 2 who will be happy to suck you dry — or at least try to pull you back to play the game their way. Don't let them do it! You might be asking, "Why would I undertake Level 3 networking if it leaves me vulnerable to others taking advantage?" Because it's the right thing to do and because the inner or psychic compensation you'll receive is worth it.

One of our coaches had been meeting, on his own time, with a young acquaintance from his former law firm to help that younger lawyer grow in various areas of his life. At one point this lawyer asked, "Given your schedule and your other commitments, why are you making the time to meet with me?" Our coach responded, "Selfishly, I feel blessed when I can help younger men grow."

Ninety-five percent of maintaining a Level 3 attitude is being intentional and making a conscious choice to network in this way. And the simple truth is that we are all capable of networking at this level. When you do, it's inevitable that more success will come your way naturally.

As you read this chapter, are you wondering whether you're a Level 3 networker? It's difficult, if not impossible, to operate at this level all the time. If you can network at Level 3 from 90 to 95 percent of the time, you will stand out. But you'll never end up doing it by accident.

In addition to the depth of the connections you will form, your self-awareness will also increase. It will become painfully obvious how often you don't want to network at Level 3. And that is valuable information to possess about yourself.

It's easy to say you'll network in this way, but it's very difficult to actually do it most of the time. What do you say? Our *challenge* to you is to give it a try for one week and see how it feels. What do you have to lose?

Learn as much as possible from people in your network;
then share what you've learned.

17

INCREASING THE VALUE OF
YOUR NETWORK

How Do Great Rainmakers Increase the Value
of Their Networks?

In our work with professionals from around the globe, we've observed that great rainmakers seek to increase the value of their networks. They do this by increasing the number of meaningful relationships within their networks. Quantity alone is meaningless.

What is the quality of the relationship you have with each person on your contacts list? Like great rainmakers, you too can look for opportunities to build better, more meaningful relationships with people. They do this in three principal ways that you can use, too:

1. Learn as much as possible from people, and then share what you're learning with others.

2. Connect people you know.

3. Spend more time with connectors.

LEARN AND SHARE

A great way to add value to your network is to learn as much as possible from every person you meet. This approach is rarely used accidentally and, when used purposefully, offers considerable benefits to you. Suppose your ideal client is a lawyer who works in-house and you know 20 people who fit that description. If you meet regularly with each of those 20 people and ask simple open-ended questions like, "What keeps you awake at night?" or "How do you tell a great general counsel from a good one?" you'll start to learn more about how in-house lawyers think and what's important to them.

More importantly, you become more valuable and knowledgeable to them as you meet in sequence with these 20 people. You might or might not gain great insights from the first few persons you try this with. But, collectively you could learn a number of things from persons 1 through 10 (insights about their jobs and work) that you can share in your meeting with person number 11. The more you learn from each person, the sharper your questions become and the more insights you can provide. If you do this systematically, you'll find that most people will fight you for the check when you meet for lunch.

The same holds true if you know a handful of business owners, another category of contacts many professionals want as part of their networks. Again, think in terms of the cumulative effect of these meetings. You might not be all that savvy after meeting with the first business owner in your network, but with some preparation and thoughtful questions, you may become very valuable by the fifth meeting with a business owner in your network. Much of your value can be attributed to the learning that occurred in the first four meetings. Not only that, but when you go back to meet with business owner number 1 for a second time, you will be more valuable to her than you were in your first visit because of the five other meetings you have under your belt.

It is amazing the number of clients who have asked me, "What do I have of value to offer to this CEO?" Notice I haven't even mentioned intent to generate business from these contacts.

That is not the goal. The goal is to learn from every contact and to share something of value with those contacts.

CONNECT PEOPLE YOU KNOW

Plant lots of seeds. Over the years, we've heard many stories of rainmakers who happened upon one or two relationships that ended up becoming significant sources for their businesses. But the best rainmakers usually work to put other people together for their mutual benefit without seeking to monetize their contacts.

One of our clients, an estate lawyer, was eager to apply the Maraia "Work for the Room" approach at a recent retirement party. Her high-energy question during the party was, "What passion would you pursue if you were retiring?" Not only did the answers make for interesting conversation, but one of her clients, a banker, told her about his passion for cooking and his upcoming catering job . . . his first. The estate lawyer was able to connect the banker with another of her clients who was stressed about feeding a large family group coming to her lake home. This particular lawyer shared what she learned and connected people. In her words, this was a "win/win/win situation."

How frequently and freely do you share your contacts with others? If your answer is "infrequently," perhaps it's time to start doing that with a purpose. I often encourage clients to "put people together for their mutual benefit." While it may seem obvious to some, putting people together by sharing information that might be beneficial to them is one way to do that. This practice will allow you to grow the value of your network.

SPEND MORE TIME WITH CONNECTORS

The next time you look through your contacts list, ask yourself: "Which people in my network seem to have the most extensive and robust networks?" These are the people who know everyone. Once you identify those people (and they will be relatively few in number), take the next step and meet with them. You can go in one of two directions during the meeting. You can try to become close enough to them and valuable enough to them that they freely make their network available to you, or you can find out how they grew their networks and learn how to apply these ideas yourself. The second option is far more valuable, and more likely to happen. Wouldn't you rather be a connector than to be dependent on one?

WHERE CAN I START?

Try starting with friends or acquaintances who are now in the kinds of firms or companies you'd target. Remember, you're not selling, you are learning. If you can't lean on your friends for some learning, who can you lean on? Meet with a friend for practice. You will be amazed at what you'll learn when your intention is to increase the value of your network rather than just generate business.

A colleague shared with me that, six years after leaving private practice, he hadn't been approached by any of his former partners seeking to learn from his six years of experience as general counsel for a large corporation. But a relatively new associate — who wasn't with the firm when he left — sought him out to learn from his experiences. What do you think the chances are of that associate becoming a good rainmaker?

If you ask great questions,
you won't have to toot your own horn.

$$\boxed{18}$$

COMPETING WITH GIANTS

How Do I Keep My Clients Forever and Keep
My Competition at Bay?

We are often asked how small firms can compete with
larger firms. We are also asked by large regional firms
how to compete against the national or international
firms. Here are nine ideas on competing with larger firms. No
matter what your size, there is almost always someone bigger (or
better known) whom you are competing against. Even if you're
with a larger firm, these ideas will give you ideas on how to keep
your clients in the fold forever and your competition at bay.

Our best advice is to build on your advantages. There might
be more than you think. Two very real advantages a smaller firm
has are nimbleness and flexibility. You can act and respond to a
client's needs much more quickly than a larger firm with its com-
mittees and review processes.

Nine Ideas When Competing with Larger Firms

1. Solicit feedback from every buyer of your services who has
ever hired bigger firms (possible titles of those buyers include

71

CEO, CFO, general counsel, and vice president of human resources, to name a few).

Find out what these buyers think the national firms bring to the table that you don't. Your existing clients will often possess key insights on how to compete against bigger firms. When you succeed in landing a client who considered using a national firm but instead chose you, find out what motivated the client to break from the national firm mold! Do this every time and you'll build a database of what sets you apart. Here are some specific questions you can ask clients:

- Is there something firm X brings to the table that we can't?

- How does the work we do for you compare to the work done by firm X?

- Who is your best outside service provider and what can we learn from him or her?

- What are some creative alternative fee arrangements you have with other firms that you'd like to explore with us?

- What's the most attractive billing arrangement you've seen between an outside service provider and her client?

In addition to asking these questions of existing clients who have worked with the big firms, don't overlook soliciting this same feedback from your friends, family, and acquaintances who serve in these same roles. In one case, our client had a neighbor who could provide insight on her use of name players. In another, it was a college classmate.

2. PLAY WELL AS A TEAM AND YOU'LL RUN CIRCLES AROUND EVERYONE. One of the greatest untapped resources in almost any firm is its ability to serve the client's needs as a team. This skill is not easy to replicate, yet it is one of the most distinct ways to stand out in the market. To do it well requires a change in how your firm (or practice group) is governed and run. The best iterations of team that we see are weekly meetings with all profes-

sionals who serve the client to discuss what's going on and how to best serve the client. Oh, and this has to been done off the clock.

Consider inviting your client to a team meeting. After the shock wears off, he will be thrilled to attend. This is a great way to keep the clients you have and to solicit advice from them about how to add others. Again, your client is well positioned to help you learn how to organize as a team to make it easier for him or her to do business with you.

3. SHOW THAT YOU ARE A SAFER CHOICE THAN NATIONAL FIRMS. You might list matters you've handled with enough detail for the client to know that your firm has represented top-tier companies and possesses such sophistication. Ideally, you can detail times when you've outsmarted the national firms that were on the other side of a deal or matter.

4. OFFER YOUR FIRST-STRING PLAYERS. Learn whether the client has ever been burned by dealing with second-string players at national firms. Also find out how the client was personally impacted by having to deal with the second-stringers. Even if your client hasn't had a bad experience with second-stringers, make sure to stress that he will get your firm's *first*-stringers.

5. ASK BETTER, MORE THOUGHTFUL QUESTIONS. "Whoever asks the best questions wins." Most people do not like tooting their own horns. If you ask great questions, you won't have to toot your own horn. During a beauty contest, one lawyer asked such thoughtful questions that his prospect said, "Why hasn't my current counsel asked me these questions?"

6. USE EXTRANETS THAT GIVE YOUR CLIENTS 24/7 ACCESS TO YOUR WORK PRODUCT. A recent client who was employed in a smaller firm asked for feedback from a desirable client and learned that a larger firm offered use of its extranets. With the proper use of extranets, you can act like a very large firm, even if you are only a five-person firm.

7. BE MORE CREATIVE WITH YOUR FEES. Move away from standard fee arrangements such as the billable hour and instead use alternative fees that have your firm putting some skin in the game. This is another question you can ask of clients while you're gathering feedback as suggested above. You might ask, "What is the most creative or appealing fee arrangement you've ever heard about?"

8. GIVE MORE BUSINESS ADVICE AWAY UP-FRONT. Too many firms of all sizes are stingy with their advice before they are hired. The way to stand out in this market is to give away great advice. And if you feel you'll give away your best advice in a few minutes, you're probably not as good as you think you are.

9. REQUEST WRITTEN TESTIMONIALS FROM CLIENTS WITH PROFILES OF THE TYPE OF CLIENT YOU WANT. It's much easier to let your clients do the selling for you.

There are times when clients will hire your more formidable competitor. However, by following all the ideas in this chapter, you will be well positioned to "compete with giants."

Do you convey the feeling to your client that you are the most important thing on his agenda that day or that he is the most important thing on your agenda?

19

NETWORKING AT DEEPER LEVELS

How Can I Improve My Odds of Meeting
with People?

Make a point of getting to know your contacts at a much deeper level. This requires making your best referral sources, top prospects, and clients feel they are the most important things on your agenda.

Frankly, not many people take the time to be thoughtful. Putting others' needs before your own might seem impossible with the demanding schedules professionals have today. It stands to reason that people in our networks have busy periods during the year when they are operating at 110 percent of capacity. . . when they are busier than usual. When a message to your client goes unreturned, it's natural to become frustrated. Some people might even take offense, which is the *worst* thing you can do.

Taking the time to learn when those busy and slow periods fall on the calendar of your clients and best contacts can be very helpful in improving your odds of meeting with people and deepening relationships.

Do you know the busy seasons for your top referral sources or your top prospects? For example, the last quarter of the year is budget season for many companies. You may find that some contacts will ignore you during this period because they're involved in an all-consuming budget process. Likewise, do you know the slow periods for your top referral sources and your top prospects?

If you can't answer these questions: First, contact your referral's assistant and ask these same questions. Most assistants have great insights on the answers to these questions. Then select two or three people who are really important for you to connect with and make a point of trying to meet with them during their slow seasons. An obvious example of this is to try reaching an accountant in May, June, or July. And perhaps just as importantly, stay out of their way during their busy seasons.

Once you know the times of year your top contacts are more available, you will have more success in actually reaching them. Making time for them when they have time allows you to deepen the connection.

Our clients find that the more they network *with* a purpose, the more time others want to spend with them. The more time spent with people, the better the relationship. The better the relationship, the more referrals and business you will see drop into your lap. And if done well, this will take pressure off your selling skills.

An estate lawyer discovered the value of spending some non-billable time with a client. She spent an hour off the clock explaining a very complex estate planning technique to a loan officer who does huge loans. This lawyer could have easily brushed off her client with an excuse such as, "I need to get back to the office." (How many times have you heard yourself say that?) She later got a call from this loan officer to do her personal estate planning. This lawyer learned that "it's okay to give non-billable time." She reaped great rewards in two ways: getting more work and deepening her relationship with this client.

Ultimately, networking at deeper levels deepens relationships. When you make a point of showing your client he is the most important thing on your agenda, you will get to know him at a much deeper level. Soon you will find yourself in his circle of trusted advisors.

When was the last time you checked in with some referral sources and clients who deserve your follow-up? Do they know how important they are to you? Take your networking to a deeper level and call them today! (Unless it's their busy period — in which case, make a note in your calendar to call them when things slow down!)

Great rainmakers view the people they deal with each day as their personal classrooms.

┌─────┐
│ 20 │
└─────┘

THE THREE ROLES OF GREAT RAINMAKERS

How Do Great Rainmakers Maintain Their Client Relationships?

If you generate more work than you can personally handle, this chapter provides a framework to manage your most important client work. Understanding how great rainmakers approach their roles can help you better manage your work. Essentially, rainmakers perform three key roles in managing client work: client satisfaction officer, work satisfaction officer, and portfolio manager/trusted advisor.

1. They Function as Client Satisfaction Officers (CSOs)

Rainmakers spend a significant amount of time getting feedback from clients. As the number of timekeepers for the client increases, the role of CSO becomes increasingly critical. If someone isn't filling that role, it will be difficult, if not impossible, to keep that client for the long term. It's risky to assume that all team members know what it takes to thrill the client, and it's impossible to ask for client feedback too frequently. Here's a list of possible feedback questions you might ask:

- What do you like about how we handled that last deal/lawsuit/project?

- Is there anything you want us to do differently next time?

- How easy is it to do business with our firm?

- If a colleague of yours called asking for a reference, what would you say to him or her about us?

- Who from the team would you like to see more of or less of?

- How well are we doing at keeping up with your business and industry?

- During the past year, what's one of the most impressive things you've seen an outside professional do for you or your company?

After you obtain client feedback, be sure to act on it. One of our clients had received favorable feedback about some work her partner had done for a client. She shared that feedback with her partner and it boosted her partner's morale and confidence. She later learned that another rainmaker in her firm had received similar feedback about this partner, but had not shared it with her.

Great rainmakers relish the chance to share feedback. If the client has favorable things to say about a team or a team member, be sure to share that good news with everyone on the team. If the client has corrective or constructive feedback, be sure to share that, too! But share corrective feedback privately. I am surprised at how few rainmakers think passing along client feedback is an essential function. This leads very naturally into the next role of a great rainmaker.

2. THEY FUNCTION AS WORK SATISFACTION OFFICERS (WSOs)

Great rainmakers believe it's their job to assemble and develop the right team. One school of thought among rainmakers says the task of assembling and developing the team is best left to the practice group leader or someone else in the firm; the rainmaker's sole responsibility is to generate the work. This is a mistake. Great rainmakers aren't just passionate about developing new business; they are passionate about developing people. They know that growing their practices is synonymous with growing their people. Great rainmakers fully embrace the role of teacher.

When partners start complaining about their work, great rainmakers want to know why the partners are unhappy. One rainmaker received a compliment from his client: "You always assemble first-rate teams to do my work." The great ones go beyond assembling great teams; they alert their partners to clients they believe will be challenging or high maintenance and make sure their partners are up to the task. A simple warning to your partner can be: "This client will leave you four voicemails at 3:00 a.m. and expect an answer by 9:00 a.m. the same day." Such a warning alerts them to what they're up against. Not providing such warnings sets your partners up for failure. If your partner isn't prepared to deal with high-maintenance clients effectively, do yourself and the client a favor and find someone else to do the work. The WSO function also presumes you are adept at delegating work effectively.

3. THEY FUNCTION AS PORTFOLIO MANAGERS OR TRUSTED ADVISORS

Do your clients come to you for ideas that go well beyond your expertise? Do they think of you as a businessperson or as a specialist? A great rainmaker is viewed as having a great business mind and is a trusted advisor. To become a trusted advisor, think of all your client's problems as business problems. Every problem, no matter the cause, affects the client's business.

How often do you talk with clients about their key strategic business issues? Have you ever offered to sit through a client's strategic planning meetings at no charge to the client? As portfolio manager, a great rainmaker becomes intimately familiar with the client's industry and business. Don't be fooled into thinking you must know all the details of the matters your team is handling for the client. That will reduce your ability to serve as portfolio manager and trusted advisor.

AN ABUNDANCE MENTALITY MINDSET

Great rainmakers carry out these three roles operating with an abundance mentality. They expect the pie to grow larger for everyone. Not only do they want to see their books of business grow larger, but they genuinely want to help others grow their books too. They love helping others succeed and they always make time for it! Great rainmakers make helping others succeed their primary mission in life.

An impressive example illustrates this. One rainmaker spent more than 20 hours during year-end writing a memo explaining why a multitude of his partners deserved higher compensation. It wasn't a required task — he did it because he really wanted to do it. Needless to say, he keeps making lots of friends within his firm's partner ranks.

Great rainmakers don't sit back and rest contentedly. There are plenty of professionals, even rainmakers, who have $4 million or $5 million books of business who could be doing $10 million if they applied themselves more diligently. Are you up to the challenge to become a great rainmaker?

Even when your services are seen as a commodity,
your relationship with clients can deliver great value.

21

DELIVERING VALUE TO CLIENTS

HOW CAN I REFOCUS THE FEES DISCUSSION TO ONE ABOUT VALUE?

One of the most common gripes of professionals is that clients are no longer willing to pay the firm's fees. Years of gradual (and sometimes not so gradual) fee increases are being met with increasing resistance. In some practice areas, clients with significant purchasing power have already established an absolute ceiling on fees. For mid- to senior-level partners, this often means that they're effectively priced out of their desired market. Among the sounds of gnashing teeth and wringing hands, there is a deafening silence regarding a realistic approach to this challenge. This chapter provides a simple, yet effective, tactic to refocus your client on the value you provide, rather than the fees you charge.

THE FIRST STEP: WHAT IS YOUR ROLE?

Moving the conversation from being one about fees to one about value is an important shift to develop clients who consistently pay your fees without complaining. The first step in this process is to understand the role your work plays in your client's business. Why is he hiring you? What does he want to accomplish? It is important to remember that he wants to manage a challenge or take advantage of an opportunity. He wants to purchase real estate, lease a piece of equipment, defend intellectual property, and/or hire the best and most talented employees. He hires professionals to document the transactions, to stop others from poaching on his intellectual property, and to create policies and procedures that help identify, recruit, and retain great employees. Place your work in your client's business context and you will be a step ahead of most professionals.

The Second Step: What Does the Client Value?

The second step is to determine what your client values about you and your work. Notice that we recommend you learn what your client values about you and about the work you do. Many clients value accuracy, a well-defined scope of work, speed, and cost-effectiveness, to name a few factors. However, your competitors may readily duplicate these factors, thus eliminating any distinction between your work and their work. In this instance, your work has become a commodity. In many areas of the country and in many areas of specialization, your clients already perceive your work to be a commodity. Don't waste your time fighting this perception. Your work might be perceived as a commodity, but you do not need to be perceived that way. That is the reason you must learn what your client values about you besides your work. Clients might value your business judgment, your ability to manage your budget so there are no surprises, or your uncanny knack for finding clients, capital, or other resources desperately sought by your client.

How can we discover what clients value? Ask them! Ask your clients for feedback on every project you do for them. Don't wait for the marketing survey, which won't occur as quickly as you need to stay on top of what's most important to your clients. Don't assume you know what your clients value because you have not received a complaint. What a client values is quite often different from what you think he values. Outside of mind-reading, the only way to know is to ask your client for feedback on a consistent basis. Your client's comments are a roadmap. Use it to consistently provide great value. The best time to obtain this roadmap is before you begin an engagement. Find out what your client values before you even begin a project.

THE FINAL STEP: EXAMINE AND MODIFY YOUR BUSINESS PRACTICES

The final step in this process is to examine your business practices and modify them as necessary so that you are actually providing what your client values with each and every project you do. Avoid the trap of simply doing excellent work. That neither sets you apart from your competition nor satisfies your client in the long run. But this step is easier said than done. One general counsel complained that outside counsel would reduce a six- or seven-figure bill by 10 percent without much more than a simple request. However, the same firm billed the general counsel $500 to $2,500 for annoying but important little projects that the general counsel occasionally needed but lacked the internal resources to complete. Think about how much value the law firm could have provided by learning what was important to this general counsel and simply completing the occasional small project as a courtesy. The firm would likely receive fewer requests for write-offs on their bills for larger matters.

A final example illustrates the power of providing real value to your client and the benefits it can provide you and your firm. One of our clients, an associate who practices in the intellectual property arena, had successfully increased her client's spending on legal fees without eliciting complaints. The lawyer listened carefully to her client and learned as much as possible about the business. She noticed that historically the company had a lax attitude about patent prosecutions. The company's prior law firm had averaged three to four patent prosecutions a year. She educated the company's executives about the business risks inherent in relying on proprietary technology and the importance of protecting its intellectual property to sustain its competitive advantage. In the next year, more than 30 patent prosecutions had been pursued. This change in business practice (and corresponding jump in legal expenditures) did not result from a change in strategic direction or a change in corporate leadership. It resulted because a lawyer took the time to learn her client's business and discovered what her client valued. She reduced the client's risk and became a true business partner who understood the business and was committed to its success.

Value is in the eye of the beholder. Learn what your client values, then consistently deliver that to him or her. You will find yourself having far fewer conversations about your fees and far more conversations about how you are helping to grow the business.

The more you think and act like your clients,
the more you inspire confidence.

$$\boxed{\textbf{22}}$$

INSPIRING CLIENT CONFIDENCE

How Do Rainmakers Build Trust?

One of the traits of all great rainmakers is the ability to inspire clients' confidence in their abilities. If a client doesn't have confidence in you, your chances of getting business from the client are slim to none. What can you do to inspire confidence? Consider these things:

Have the Answers on the "Top of Your Head"

Rainmakers are not afraid to give advice and answers to a client's questions on the spot. A senior partner and rainmaker who recently left his firm to pursue other passions saw two former clients at the next table at lunch one day. When he stopped to say hello, they volunteered that they really missed having him at the firm, and one said, "When I called, you always had the answer on the top of your head." What the client was really saying was that when he asked a question, he received an immediate answer.

This is not to suggest that rainmakers are cavalier and give unreasoned advice, but it does suggest that rainmakers have enough confidence in themselves that they can, and do, give clients ready answers to their questions. The sense of confidence the client gains from these encounters is palpable. If the rainmaker doesn't have the answer, she's also not afraid to say, "I don't know," immediately followed by, "but I'll find out the answer and get back to you." And, she does! That's another thing you can do to inspire confidence. Always follow through on your promises.

When you don't know the answer and your client doesn't have the luxury of time to let you find out, use the question as a chance to "think out loud." This lets the client into your thought process. If he likes the factors you consider and the subtleties you pick up on, it can put you in his trusted advisor camp very quickly.

CLIENTS DON'T HAVE LEGAL PROBLEMS, THEY HAVE BUSINESS PROBLEMS

Rainmakers who are lawyers know instinctively that clients don't categorize problems they encounter into legal and non-legal problems. They only have business problems with legal implications. One lawyer's primary client contact was an experienced chief financial officer (CFO). This CFO would call his lawyer for advice on business issues and start with, "I know this isn't a legal issue, but...."

When a client asks for advice outside your technical area of expertise, she should get the advice. Don't give a response such as, "That's a business issue, not a legal issue." While the client's issue may be one that doesn't have a specific legal solution, it is a problem for the client and she has asked for advice from the person in whom she has confidence and trust: her lawyer. When that happens, the successful lawyer gives the advice.

Rainmakers also think beyond the issue at hand to determine what impact their advice will have on their client's business. Telling a client all the reasons why he shouldn't do something isn't helpful if the client needs that particular thing to be done. The professional who inspires client confidence is the one who realizes the business needs to progress and helps the client find the best way to make it happen.

Know as Much About the Client's Business as She Does

You might be thinking, "How can I possibly know as much about my client's business as she does? I'm not there all the time running it." Rainmakers take the time to learn as much about a client's business as they can, so they can inspire confidence with their knowledge of the client's business.

A general counsel of one company with more than 900 employees was surprised to hear his boss, the CFO, tell him, "You know more about our business than all but me and the president." That general counsel had been hired from private practice because he had represented the corporation and made it his practice to learn as much about the client's business practices, procedures, and pricing models as he possibly could. That depth of knowledge shows that the lawyer truly cares about his client's business and its success, which inspires client confidence.

Take it one step further and make it your business to know as much as possible about your client's customers. That will really inspire confidence and trust in you.

Make the Client's Job (and Life) Easier

When one professional reviews a contract for clients, she makes it a practice not only to give comments on what she is reviewing but to suggest the changes that need to be made, including the actual language changes to the documents. Another partner in the same firm wrote the client a seven-page letter with comments on the contract, but failed to offer any concrete suggestions on how to make it acceptable.

Not surprisingly, the client wants to do business with the partner who offers specific language rather than seven-page memos. Which professional do you think inspires the most confidence in the client? The one who makes the client's life easier, of course.

HELP YOUR CLIENTS ACHIEVE CLARITY AROUND
WHAT THEY NEED

Professionals who can distinguish between a client's needs and wants, and can satisfy them both, will inspire confidence. Clients often want something vastly different from what they need. In fact, many times the wants obscure the needs so much that clients are oblivious to what they need. For example, you might receive a call from a client asking to have a contract drafted that, when fully described, turns out to be a joint venture agreement, and not a contract.

Wouldn't it be great if every associate were pulled aside on his or her first day on the job and instructed to focus on inspiring client confidence? There is no more valuable yet amorphous skill. Professionals who inspire their clients' confidence attain other desirable outcomes such as client satisfaction, fierce loyalty, and repeat business.

Taking notes during a meeting conveys
respect to the speaker.

23

TAKING NOTES CAN MAKE YOU STAND OUT

HOW DOES NOTE-TAKING GIVE ME AN ADVANTAGE
IN RELATIONSHIPS?

Many professionals fail to take a single note during conversations with prospective clients. Making mental note of what is said is nice, but it won't last as long as a written note. Going note-less is a huge disadvantage, and you miss an opportunity to make a great impression in your next call or meeting.

If you met with a client to discuss her project and didn't take a single note, what does the client think about you as a professional? Why should meetings with prospective clients be any different? Obviously, there might be situations for which note-taking wouldn't be important or easy, but a lot fewer than most people think. If you are meeting someone in a conference room where it's easy to take notes, then do so. If you're not sure how the client will react, simply ask for permission. Say something like, "You are making some very interesting points. Would you mind if I make some notes?" Almost anyone will be flattered that you think enough of what he is saying to take notes.

Many professionals assume they shouldn't take notes while sharing a meal with a prospective client, while others simply don't know whether it is appropriate. Quite frankly, it depends. You must rely on your common sense. If the table space doesn't permit it, then don't attempt it. If the table is big enough, or you can manage to take notes in your lap, then go for it.

Keeping electronic notes is better than handwritten ones because electronic notes are hard to misplace, and you can usually retrieve, manipulate, and annotate electronic notes more easily than written notes. However, using a paper-based note-taking system is far better than nothing.

WHY NOTE-TAKING HAS VALUE

The value of taking notes during meetings is unimpeachable. Clients and prospects say many things worth writing down. If you don't write them down as you hear them, you will eventually forget them. Research shows we forget up to 90 percent of what we hear within a short period of time. The level of detail you remember is limited when all you have is your memory. The old adage applies that the weakest link is stronger than the mightiest memory.

Note-taking also allows you to pick up a conversation where you left off, even if there has been a six-month gap with your contact. For example, the prospect might tell you she plans to put this work out for bid next year. Four months later you can ask if she's done so. Or she might tell you she is going on vacation to Fiji. Your first question might be, "How was your vacation in Fiji?"

If taking notes isn't an option during your meeting, budget 10 to 15 minutes after the meeting (or as soon as possible) to write down the salient facts discussed. Noting what needs were mentioned will help you remember your client's personal needs, which is more likely to swing the sale in your direction. If you really want to zoom to the top, annotate your notes. This involves going back through your notes to flag the needs you wrote down. Either way, make sure you go back over your notes and identify the needs you jotted down on paper.

For really important meetings, you might annotate your previous notes by marking which needs are implied and which are explicit. Implied needs are statements of dissatisfaction with no stated desire for solutions, such as "I'm not happy with my current provider." Explicit needs are statements of dissatisfaction and a stated desire for solutions, such as "We are looking for new counsel because my current firm isn't getting the job done."

Don't take notes for the sake of taking notes. If getting the client has minimal appeal, don't bother with notes. Take notes for the clients you want to get and keep. You will stand out to prospective clients because so few people take notes and even fewer make those notes an integral part of their relationship-building strategy. Note-taking, if done well, can gain you an enormous competitive advantage, and all professionals are well served to do so. It really is a nonverbal way of saying, "You are important enough to me that I am writing down what you say."

If you're feeling overwhelmed, empower your assistant
to do triage for you.

24

EMPOWER YOUR ASSISTANT

How Can a Triage Approach to Handling Calls Improve My Relationships?

Many professionals we coach feel overwhelmed in their practices at some point or another. You know the feeling of being besieged by work. You're inundated by too many phone calls, too much work, or too many meetings. When this happens, files pile up on your desk, phone calls go unreturned, deadlines are missed, and late nights become a staple in your work. Frustration, anxiety, concern, resentment, and even anger can accompany this feeling.

When was the last time you felt overwhelmed? What did you do about it? When there is too much on your plate, trying to handle it by yourself is unwise because it leads to greater misery.

So Many Calls, So Little Time

One of our clients is an estate planning lawyer who was fielding dozens of client calls and messages every day. She was nearly overwhelmed with phone messages and asked her coach for ideas. She eventually solved her problem in part by making her assistant an integral player in her service delivery team.

Her problems started to multiply when she was out of the office for an extended period of time and was unable to retrieve voice messages. Upon her return she learned, to her horror, that many of her voice messages had been deleted by the firm's automated phone system!

In addition to working with the firm's facility experts to set up her voice message system differently, she created a process in which her assistant checks her voice messages every four hours and is empowered to return calls on her behalf. This new system, or triage approach, reduces her volume of messages by 50 percent because her assistant is able to resolve most issues without attorney involvement.

Those messages that can't be resolved by her assistant fall into two categories: issues needing immediate action and those that can wait. Issues in the first category are rare, but when they happen her assistant notifies her by e-mail if she's in court or at a meeting. For the less urgent messages, her assistant pulls the file for her so she knows what the client is calling about and has the relevant materials waiting on her desk so she can respond as time allows.

When her usual assistant is out of the office, she implements a simpler version of this same process using a temporary employee. She has the temp transcribe all of the messages and pull the necessary files. This isn't as smooth as using her long-time assistant, but it still saves her time and lets her prioritize the calls.

This triage approach to handling the high volume of calls reduces the amount of traffic she has to manage, helps her prioritize the calls, reduces her stress level, and has taken a huge burden off her shoulders. Ironically, this has also allowed her to delegate more work to her assistant.

The new process works wonderfully and allows her to increase her own service levels. She now calls clients twice for each message they leave her, which demonstrates an unmatched level of responsiveness. Clients love it. And they aren't offended by a call-back from the assistant. In the long run, clients understand that this process helps them too because it keeps the work moving forward and they are kept more firmly in the loop. She estimates the new process saves her an hour per day, which she reinvests in more billable work and more relationship building.

ARE YOU FEELING OVERWHELMED?

If you are feeling overwhelmed, perhaps you should consider learning from our client's success. But don't delay. . .your stress and workload only get worse when you fail to change.

Make it your mission to inspire client confidence in your team.

24

BUILDING YOUR TEAM'S CREDIBILITY

HOW CAN I BUILD TEAM CREDIBILITY AND INSPIRE CLIENT CONFIDENCE?

If you're not actively working to increase the credibility of your team, then you're most likely doing things to undermine it. A simple example makes this point. Your best client calls your office with a question, but you're not there to answer it. What happens? Does your client talk to another member of your team or does he leave a message asking you to call him back? When you find yourself fielding questions that could be answered by more junior members of your team, you could be guilty of promoting the client behavior. It also increases your burdens and pressures.

Many professionals become victims of their own success. We have become addicted to being needed and sought after by our clients, even when the work needed from us is not challenging or inspiring. Ask all your team members: "If a client called you with a question you couldn't answer, what would you say?" Their answers may surprise you.

Too often what the client hears is "Let me ask [Your Name]." Eliminate that kind of response from your team members! We've worked with many partners who were able to save a dozen hours a week by instructing their staff to avoid this kind of language. Such a response implies that your team members are too green or unfamiliar with your business. It hardly inspires confidence.

To inspire client confidence, ask your team members to be very careful with their language around clients. Discourage phrases like "Let me ask [Your Name]" and "Let me check with [More Senior Partner]." This latter phrase is more likely to be used by newer partners who haven't made the transition to a partner mindset.

There are also phrases that you can use more, such as "I don't know, but let me ask [Your Valued Associate], who's really more familiar with this subject than I am" and "[Your Valued Associate] is exceptional at answering your question. Let's see if she can meet with you now." The whole point of using these phrases is to build up your team in the client's mind. We want the client to think your associate is better qualified than you.

Include secretaries and other assistants as an integral part of your team, too. If you regularly provide clients with work and home phone numbers, be sure your entire staff provides theirs as well. Keep your assistant in the loop about developments in the matter.

During a recent coaching session with a lawyer, it was clear he was passionate about developing a practice representing people in the entertainment industry and had acquired several well-known clients in that business. At the same time, he had just received a new client with a tremendous number of new matters in another area that were going to take up most of his time. He told me his plan was to spend six to eight months developing the client relationship before handing the work off to a very capable associate in his firm. His coach discouraged him from waiting six months to begin shedding the work. He embarked on transitioning the work to his team immediately and was very glad he did.

What a shame it would have been if this work had side-tracked him for six to eight months, draining his energies and his enthusiasm for practicing law. He quickly realized that his ticket to doing the work he loves is to build up his team. The more effectively you transition work to your team, the less you must do personally and the more free time you will have for higher-value and fun activities. Your team will also reward your confidence in them.

PART IV

Making More Time for Relationships

*The amount of time you spend marketing
depends on your goals.*

26

DEVOTING HOURS TO BUSINESS DEVELOPMENT

HOW MUCH TIME SHOULD I SPEND MARKETING?

From time to time we are asked how many hours per week professionals should devote to business development at the various stages of their careers, especially as associates. Most people want to know what the norms are, but there really aren't any norms. To quote Cleat Simmons, one of our coaches, "Too many people approach marketing with a one-size-fits-all mentality."

As a rule, it is misleading to set forth a number of hours one should devote to business development. This is true for several reasons.

WHAT'S YOUR GOAL?

First, your goal will be different from another professional's goal. If you want to generate seven figures' worth of business but you're only investing two hours a week on business development activities, you won't achieve your goal. By contrast, the individual who doesn't have a business development goal won't spend two hours a week on business development activities.

QUALITY OF INTERACTIONS

Business development is about building relationships. It's nearly impossible to put a purely quantitative standard on such an activity because relationship building is about the quality of each interaction. One associate can easily spend 10 hours every week on some form of business development and accomplish little or nothing. Without interacting with people — former classmates, potential referral sources, and future decision-makers — most of it is wasted time and effort. By contrast, another associate can spend two hours per week establishing her network and be well on her way to building a solid foundation for future business.

Your business development activities increase in value when you add quality interaction with people. For example, if you want to write an article for publication, you could ask a couple of your clients or referral sources for their opinions on the topic you want to cover. If you call three people, not only will they be flattered to be quoted, but you will also have increased the value of your relationship with each and will likely improve the quality of your article.

VALUE OF ACTIVITY

Just as important as your goal and the quality of your interactions is the value of the activity you undertake. Some business development activities are far more likely to produce results than others.

Before heading into an activity, determine the value of the activity. For example, if you are thinking about attending a conference, ask yourself these questions to evaluate its quality: Is the conference attended mostly by competitors or will it be well attended by prospects? What are my goals for the conference? Who else (clients, prospects, etc.) is planning to attend the conference?

Once you've determined that an activity is worth doing, leverage your involvement in that activity to build on existing or desired relationships. For example, you will have already determined that speaking to an audience of prospective clients is far more useful and valuable than speaking to an audience filled with your competitors or your peers. To maximize the value of a speaking engagement, call on some clients to let them know you're making a presentation, ask them what they'd like to hear if they were attending (which will more than likely enhance your presentation), and be sure to follow up with those in the audience after the talk.

Play to Your Strengths

Are you choosing business development activities that play to your strengths? If you love public speaking and hate writing articles, do more speaking and less writing.

If you like group events, attend them. If you don't, find another activity that fits you better. We have coached many professionals who have attended group events. Some have met many great prospects at these functions; others have never met a single prospect at a group event. From a purely quantitative perspective, if an individual who has never met a prospect at a group event is spending six hours each month attending group events, it is a total waste of time. If that same individual is able to generate ten meaningful connections from one speaking engagement, then he is well advised to do more speaking gigs!

Focus on activities you enjoy and do well as a means for building your practice. It is axiomatic that if you're doing something you enjoy, you will be better at it, and other people will recognize that. One of our coaches was working with a young partner who enjoyed volunteering with Habitat for Humanity, but wondered whether that was a good use of his time. His enthusiasm for Habitat was apparent. Our coach encouraged continued participation, knowing that the outcome will be that the young partner will be happier doing something he really enjoys; others will pick up on that and be more likely to seek that partner's services because of his enthusiastic attitude.

Integrate Business Development into Your Daily Life

How attuned are you to business development during your daily life? Most professionals find themselves at events that provide rich marketing opportunities, but they don't recognize those events as marketing opportunities. For example, the individual who stands along the sidelines of her son's soccer game each week and always asks other parents high-energy questions is far more productive with her time (not marketing time, just time) than the person who doesn't even know what the other parents do for a living. That time counts for a great deal in the first instance, and counts for almost nothing in the latter.

One of our clients was a lateral partner who commuted by ferry to his office each day. This lawyer had been doing this for several years and was under extreme pressure to produce business. After a moderate amount of self-reflection and analysis of what was already working for him, he realized that some of his best prospects were generated from getting to the ferry parking lot and just missing the earlier ferry. In other words, he did some of his best marketing while commuting to work! He also began following up more systematically with those same people. While this example is unique to this client, it is not unique to your opportunity to play to your strengths and unique circumstances.

FOCUS ON FUN

One final thought to consider: If you engage in activities that are enjoyable and fun, you won't be counting the hours you spend marketing.

Instead of counting hours, we encourage many clients to begin a journal or log that spells out the business development actions they've taken each week. Doing this serves as a great reminder to make relationship building a priority and will be a great resource in determining where you are most effective.

It also proves useful at the end of the year when the firm asks what contributions you've made in the business development arena. You can whip out your log and say, "I'm really glad you asked me that question. . . ."

*View the time you spend marketing as
an investment in your future.*

┌─────┐
│ 27 │
└─────┘

INVEST YOUR MARKETING
TIME WISELY

How Can I Make Time for Marketing?

One of the most frequently asked questions we hear from professionals is, "How can I budget my marketing time?" They usually proceed to explain how many hours they bill each month and how many hours of marketing they do each month. Some clients ask this question to compare how they are doing against others. That is a wasted exercise. There is no magic ratio. How much time you invest in relationship building will differ depending on your goal and your level of effectiveness. For example, if you are investing 10 hours per month marketing, but you want to generate a $2 million book of business, you are not likely to reach your goal. So the first question you must ask yourself is, "What is my goal for marketing?" If your goal is simply to keep your own plate filled with work, that is one goal. Some professionals view that as gaining greater control of their own destinies. If your goal is to keep your own plate filled with interesting work, that is a different goal entirely. If your goal is to generate enough work to keep three people busy, that will almost certainly require more relationship-building time.

While some people might have relationship-building goals that require more time to achieve them, for the vast majority of professionals, the key is to invest time more wisely. You don't have to spend more time marketing. However, you will need to make more effective use of the time you devote to marketing. To put it bluntly, not every hour invested in relationship building is as effective or the same as every other hour spent marketing. The person who spends ten hours in one month writing a speech will be nowhere near as effective as another person who invests three hours talking to clients before a presentation about a topic she is presenting, three hours on her presentation, and another four hours following up with clients and prospects after she speaks.

The key to effective and wise use of marketing time is building relationships. In the first situation above, the professional had done very little to build relationships. By contrast, that is primarily what the second professional is doing. In addition, she is far more likely to have a dynamic presentation because she tried her ideas out on the audience before the actual presentation.

Some professionals are so reactive about marketing that they never set aside any time for doing it. Try setting a weekly appointment with yourself on your calendar. Set the appointment for the same day and time each week if your schedule permits. The key is to block out time every week. Make sure it says "business development" or something similar to remind you of the reason, and then keep the appointment! Like any important activity, you must *make* time for building relationships. Too often we wait to see whether there is any extra time in the day for marketing. If you do that, there never will be.

EFFECTIVE MARKETING

Effective marketing time will have greater return on investment (ROI) when focused on relationships. Many professionals spend time without considering this in the process. These two lists demonstrate the kinds of activities that deliver minimal and maximum return on your invested marketing time.

Ineffective Marketing Activities

- Attend the local professional association meeting if most of your referrals *do not* come from professionals like yourself.

- Spend hours preparing for and writing a speech.

- Spend hours writing an article.

- Meet with prospective clients and *tell* them how great you are or why they should hire you.

To effectively invest your marketing time in building relationships, consider this partial list of activities.

Effective Marketing Activities

- Call a dormant client to reconnect.

- Have lunch with a partner to discuss his or her ideal client.

- Call a dormant client to invite him to your upcoming speech.

- Call a dormant client to interview her for an article you are writing.

- Ask a client for feedback on your services.

- Visit a client's plant or business location off the clock.

- Meet with a friend as her trusted advisor.

- Meet with a prospective client to learn about his business.

One client became very excited when told he could make more money if he reduced the number of hours he invested in marketing but spent those hours more effectively. He was quite pleased when it happened. And he did it by spending more time in relationship-oriented activities and by eliminating non-relationship-oriented activities.

There are plenty of ways to reallocate your marketing time to obtain a better return than you're now getting. Get started today — and remember to focus on relationship-oriented activities!

Use your BlackBerry® or PDA sparingly and devote more time to relationships both within and outside the firm.

28

FIRE YOUR PDA!

How Can Turning Off My PDA Give Me More Time for Relationships?

A senior executive of a large Fortune 500 company who is responsible for driving over $1 billion in sales for his company recently told me his region was consistently ranked as the best performing region for more than seven consecutive months. When asked by co-workers what contributed to his ability to deliver such stellar results, he said, "I fired my BlackBerry." Since he turned in his PDA, his region has been the top-performing region in the company, in spite of the hundreds of e-mails he receives every day.

If this executive had turned in his BlackBerry and ignored his business relationships, he wouldn't be the topic of this chapter. However, he has become very skilled at asking great questions to find out what his customers are thinking and why they think the way they do. Getting rid of his BlackBerry enabled him to fully focus on his relationships with internal and external customers.

Without a BlackBerry to distract him, he can give his sales team his undivided attention, and he has more time to listen and to understand how they perceive their jobs. He has more time to learn what works in one store, and when he hears a good idea from one store, he shares that success with other stores.

He travels a great deal, but being in many places has allowed him to spend more time coaching people to deliver results. He found that his BlackBerry was a distraction to building relationships. It was a distraction to have it buzzing all the time because the temptation to read the message and respond was enormous. Even if he didn't give in, the temptation and the decision to resist were competing for his attention. As a result, he fired his BlackBerry, and he's glad he did.

SHOULD YOU FIRE YOUR PDA?

We're not suggesting that everyone ditch his or her PDA. However, you might want to ask yourself whether such technology is the tail wagging the dog. Is it hindering the deepening of your relationships with clients, peers, and even family members? It's a safe bet that if a family member asks you to stop reading your BlackBerry when you're with him or her, you are probably misusing the technology.

Even if getting rid of your PDA is too Draconian for you, consider the following practices to make relationships more central to your work:

1. Don't carry it everywhere you go.

2. Switch it off during client meetings and other important meetings. When you respond to a message while meeting with someone, whether it's a client, partner, associate, or staff, you are sending non-verbal messages that say, "You aren't very important" or "You are not worth my undivided attention." Even looking at the device when it alerts you to a new message can cause your client to feel he is less significant, whether you take the time to read the message or not.

3. Don't take your PDA with you when you are not working. If you do, you are making similar non-verbal statements to your family and friends that work is more important than they are.

4. Monitor your usage. For example, if you normally keep it on twelve hours per day, try to reduce the time to only six hours per day.

5. Consider changing to a technology that requires you to download e-mails, such as a Treo™. You will still have access to your e-mail, but you can control when.

Only someone secure in his or her skills and talents can turn off or restrict PDA usage; it is only the extremely insecure ones who feel the need for it to be with them at all times. If the trend continues, we might need to start a new self-help group called "PDAs Anonymous." As my executive friend discovered, not having one has been a great way to stand out in a very competitive field. PDAs and BlackBerries are great tools for increasing productivity if used properly. If misused, they become another distraction from the primary business we are all in, which is building relationships. The real question you might ask yourself about your PDA is, "Do I control *it* or does it control *me?*"

Before you do something, always be clear about your purpose for doing it.

29

STARVED FOR TIME?
ADOPT THE 5 D'S APPROACH

HOW CAN I BE MORE PRODUCTIVE?

Whether it's that pile of work on your desk, a project to manage, an event to plan, or any other collection of tasks you have to handle, you have a choice to make before you start working.

You can simply plow into the work, starting with whatever is on top and working until you've finished. This is a tactical approach and, while your work ethic and sense of responsibility will cause you eventually to finish the work, you will likely waste time, encounter frustration, and personally handle tasks better handled differently or by someone else.

Or you can apply the 5 D's Approach to your work. This strategic approach will, without fail, make you more efficient and productive, lead to higher-quality results, and let you spend more time on things you are good at and like to do (thus, making you happier). It will sometimes even give you a chance to offer a developmental opportunity to someone else, build a relationship, or create a reusable tool.

How the 5 D's Approach Works

Instead of simply digging into work, spend a few minutes before you start to examine each piece of work to see whether it can be put into one of these five categories: *drop, defer, downsize, delegate, or do.*

D.1 — DROP. Does the work need to be done at all? Who needs it and why? How does it tie to the accomplishment of a goal or project? How does it tie to the achievement of your organization's strategic goals? If it's not necessary or valuable, drop it.

D.2 — DEFER. Does the work need to be done now? How should it be prioritized in light of the rest of your work? If it doesn't need to be done now, put it in your tickler file so that it comes back to you in time for you to finish it by its deadline. (This has the added benefit of clearing stuff off your desk.)

D.3 — DOWNSIZE. Does the work need to be done as presented, or is it really a smaller or different task when you think about it in the context of project deliverables and overall goals? If a modified or different effort would more clearly or efficiently lead to the right result, then do what actually needs to be done, rather than merely doing the work as presented or requested.

D.4 — DELEGATE. Are you the right person to do the work? Would it be better handled by someone senior (who could get the result faster), a peer (who has more expertise, experience, or time and could obtain a better or quicker result), a subordinate (because it doesn't require skills where you add value), an outside service provider (who has more bodies to throw at it, more expertise, a better process, or other tools), etc. If the right result can be more effectively achieved by someone else, enroll that someone else and delegate.

D.5 — DO. Finally, once you have dropped, deferred, downsized, and delegated work as appropriate, what's left is what you DO.

Effective delegation improves firm profits and enables team members to get up-to-speed in months rather than years.

30

OBSTACLES TO EFFECTIVE DELEGATION

WHAT STOPS ME FROM BEING AN EFFECTIVE DELEGATOR?

The professionals we coach are always seeking more rewarding, profitable, and fun work. Does that describe you? Do you spend 90 percent or more of each day doing work that's fun, rewarding, and profitable? If not, perhaps delegation is the way to achieve this "trifecta."

Effective delegation provides your firm with a competitive advantage because, when it's done well, your team members learn new skills in far less time than it takes your competitors to develop the same skills. It also removes the boring and routine work that needs to be accomplished from your plate. Given these advantages, you'd expect that effective delegation would often be found in professional service firms. This just isn't so. There are some very basic reasons for this gap. Here are the most common ones.

Hoarding Work

You hoard work because you want to keep your billable hours up. Hoarding leaves you performing tasks that are boring and routine, which is a recipe for disaster. In most cases, you will end up with unhappy clients. Clients are likely to receive bills that exceed their budget when work is hoarded, and we all know they hate those kinds of surprises. It also prevents your more junior people from gaining valuable experience and can lead to rapid turnover.

Short-Term Thinking

Many professionals won't take 30 minutes to delegate a task they could have completed in 30 minutes themselves. Unfortunately, this attitude overlooks the value in saved time by showing an associate how to complete the task. Once it has been learned, the associate can complete such a task thereafter. The amount of time saved during the course of one year is vast. Once an associate learns a task, she can take responsibility for it thereafter, saving vast amounts of time over the course of a year.

Inflated Self-Image

Most people don't identify themselves as poor delegators. When faced with the choice between admitting to poor delegation skills and finding something defective about other people, they will choose the latter. "I'm already good at delegation" is a prevailing opinion of poor delegators. Just as an alcoholic must recognize a drinking problem before getting help, so too must the poor delegator recognize he doesn't delegate well.

Lack of Role Models

Many people have not learned effective delegation skills because they never had any role models to emulate. Teaching delegation skills to people is relatively easy when the mentor has the experience and knowledge to share. However, the universe of professionals who had effective mentors is in very short supply. Unfortunately, poor delegation can be perpetuated from one generation to the next.

"I Can Do It Best" Attitude

Some people believe they can't afford to have others do the work or that others won't do the work to their standard of quality. If others aren't given the opportunity to learn how to do the work, they really won't be able to do it. A good rule to follow in deciding whether or not to delegate work is this: When another member of your team can learn to do the job at 95 percent of your level of efficacy, let him or her do it! Most perfectionists can't get past this obstacle. If you truly don't have qualified people, take a good look in the mirror. It's *your* hiring and delegation skills that are the cause of the problem.

"No One" to Delegate to

Often the only people left to do the work are too junior, which translates into more work for the delegator. In other words, the delegation won't be fast and easy. Since most professionals are already starved for time, they don't want to be the ones who develop new people. They hope someone else will train these juniors. If they do take on the task of developing others, it's done grudgingly. This keeps new people from developing skills quickly, and it leads to low morale among junior people. There are no quick fixes for effective delegation.

Lack of effective delegation creates a vicious circle. When no one delegates or takes the time to delegate, there is no one trained to accept work when the work is so overwhelming that it needs to be delegated. It is the rare person who happens to gain enough skill and experience working on her own under this system. Most often, junior people leave out of frustration, and that leaves an even bigger void in the delegation process.

If you can't surmount the obstacles above, don't plan on spending 90 percent of your day on work that is fun, rewarding, and profitable. We see very few people who would describe 90 percent of their work that way. Effective delegation has the added benefit of allowing your new hires to become self-sustaining *much sooner* than on average. In fact, the speed at which you develop your people — three months compared to one to two years — can be a distinct competitive advantage. If that doesn't grab your attention, consider this: It's another way of maximizing your firm's profits.

Delegate routine marketing tasks you don't enjoy to your assistant or your administrative or marketing staff.

31

HOW TO DELEGATE EFFECTIVELY

WHAT STEPS CAN I TAKE TO DELEGATE EFFECTIVELY?

We frequently ask our clients the question, "How much of your current workload can be done by someone else?" It's not uncommon to hear that 30 to 50 percent of the work is delegable! These same people often complain of being overworked. What usually follows is a litany of excuses. If you are unable to overcome the psychological hurdles of delegating work, be resigned to do it yourself. You are likely to be stressed and miserable and you won't be able to grow your business. However, if you are highly motivated to delegate, be sure to do it correctly.

STEPS TO DELEGATE WORK EFFECTIVELY

Here is a simple process you can go through to move work off your plate.

Step 1. Decide What Work You Want to Delegate

Think in terms of a specific project or clearly identifiable task. The more routine and time-consuming the task, the more sense it makes to delegate it. If you're swamped with work, you will want to delegate the project that is the most labor-intensive. The more

123

hours you can off-load, the better. If you can't off-load the whole project, delegate those portions that can be done by others. Potentially, this will save you hundreds of hours.

One real estate partner negotiated a deal for his client. Once the deal was done, it required doing five similar deals using the prototype documents he had just negotiated. He did the first deal, but also involved a second-year associate. He devoted 100 hours to the first deal and instructed his associate extensively. Working with the same associate, he spent only 30 hours of his time on the second deal and little time at all on the final three deals. In total, this partner could have spent 500 hours on these deals. Instead, he invested 130 hours and saved 370 hours.

Many of our clients are surprised when asked whether there are any routine marketing tasks they can off-load. This ends up being the blinding flash of the obvious to some, and they are thrilled to off-load routine marketing tasks like updating their list of referral sources and other contacts. One of our clients complained of her office being so filled with old files and other stuff that she could barely work at her desk. She began meeting with her assistant once per week to clear old files out of her office. Within about four weeks, she had shipped out 15 boxes! She felt elated about that success and her productivity soared.

We had a rainmaker who received 20 requests per year to speak at conferences without pay. She had habitually accepted all speaking requests. While that might have made sense when she was a rising star, she no longer had the time for ALL of them. The best delegators are happy to send partners and associates in their places. This rainmaker saved an enormous amount of time by speaking at three of the 20 events and passed along the other 17 opportunities to several other people in her firm.

Step 2. Determine the Best Person to Handle This Project

Identify who can potentially handle the project. Recognize that the most experienced person may find the work just as uninteresting as you do and may also be oversubscribed for work, just like you. Instead, assign the project to someone who is eager to learn and would find the work interesting and challenging.

Step 3. Identify the Goal of the Project

Clearly identify the goal of the project. This includes identifying the steps needed to achieve the goal as well as gathering detailed information about the client's expectations and your own expectations. The more information you provide to your associate, the better he will grasp what's needed.

How you communicate at this stage of the delegation is critical. The more clearly you communicate what you want, the fewer glitches and surprises you'll experience. It is extremely helpful to give people the whys of the project and the big picture. In some cases, you'll need to describe the client's organizational structure in extensive detail to explain why the deal is being done a certain way.

There are many different ways to handle this step in the delegation process. You can presume she knows the steps, but this can lead to embarrassment for both of you if she doesn't admit to not understanding something — and you'll find yourself repeating instructions on every project and receiving substandard work.

You can tell her the steps verbally, but a host of presumptions are built into this method of delegation. This approach assumes that you correctly listed every step and in the correct order, and it assumes that your associate clearly understood each step. And if your associate doesn't take notes, it is unlikely she'll remember the steps. If you insist on setting forth the steps verbally, at least develop the habit of asking your associate to confirm her understanding of those steps in an e-mail.

You can provide her with written steps. At a minimum, every assignment should begin with you providing the steps to follow in writing. Don't assume this step isn't needed with experienced associates. And remember, the manner in which you convey the steps is critical. If people feel talked down to and devalued, you'll encounter steep resistance.

You can ask the associate to provide you with a list of steps. This can be done with more experienced people. Be clear that you're not testing him; you are trying to gain an understanding of his knowledge base and you hope to learn from him. When you adopt this practice with multiple people doing similar work, you learn something.

You can ask him to provide you with a list of steps and to say where he has gaps in knowledge. Checking for full understanding of the assignment is very rare. It requires a high level of trust between the delegator and the delegatee. In some cases, it isn't feasible. This approach takes more time, but it radically reduces the chances that the work will need to be redone by you.

Step 4. Establish Clear Milestones and Deadlines

Suggest interim times to assess progress. If you don't, you are setting your delegatee up for failure. Always spell out the estimated number of hours the task should take. Ask him or her to come see you if he or she is about to exceed that number of hours.

Step 5. Have a Protocol for Potential Problems

It's wise to have a protocol if problems arise that the associate can't resolve or handle on her own. There are four simple ways to deal with problems: (1) you can solve all problems, (2) you can tell your associate how to solve the problem and follow up with her, (3) you can ask your associate to solve the problem and seek your approval, or (4) you can empower your associate to take action and tell you about it afterward. The best leaders encourage their associates to take as much ownership in solving problems as possible. It communicates that you have great confidence in their skills.

Step 6. Give Your Associate Clear Feedback

If you don't give him clear feedback, he won't learn much from his experience. This feedback should be given both during and immediately after a project is completed. Feedback lets an associate know all he should about doing a certain kind of work. For example, suppose your associate handled a client project for you but you reworked it for the client without telling your associate. The associate will never learn about the need for tweaking to meet a client's requirements if you don't close the loop with him.

Step 7. Check with the Associate on Lessons Learned

Once the project is complete, be sure to check to see what lessons were learned. This step can be combined with Step 6 above. By taking time to debrief about completed work, you can allow people to come up-to-speed more rapidly. If your associate added some steps or got a great result, be sure to acknowledge her for it. Let her know *you* learned something too.

PITFALLS AND BENEFITS

Even if you follow the delegation steps perfectly, there will be pitfalls. Associates might think you only delegate the grunt work or you don't treat them with respect. You might have to step in and rework the delegated project or you might have to deal with clients on satisfaction issues. If so, it's a perfect opportunity to help solve the client's problem and let him or her know you care. You might also have to write off some time. In the long run, the benefits outweigh the pitfalls.

Effective delegation will reap great rewards such as worry-free vacations, associates who prefer to work with you because they learn more from you, and the respect of your peers and associates.

If you're not having fun or if your work seems to have become a bit too routine, perhaps the solution is to start delegating effectively. Rise to this challenge. Move five hours of uninteresting and routine work off your plate this week and keep doing that every week for the next month. You should be having more fun in no time!

Free up hundreds of hours of your time by drawing on the most underused resource in your firm — your assistant.

32

INCREASE YOUR ASSISTANT'S ROLE IN YOUR MARKETING

HOW CAN MY ASSISTANT HELP WITH MARKETING?

One of the most common complaints we hear from professionals is that they don't have enough time to focus on marketing efforts because they're too busy with their practices. Invariably, we discover that a client could delegate at least 10 percent of the work on his or her plate at any given moment, but never does so. For most professionals, their delegable work includes firm administration, marketing, and even professional development activities. This chapter focuses on the most underused resource in almost every professional's life — his or her assistant.

To get the most out of a partnership with an assistant, there is a critical shift in thinking that most professionals will need to make before trying the three-step process outlined here. You will never get the best from your assistant if you think of him solely as someone who answers your phone and types your documents. Shift your thinking and start considering him as a partner in your marketing and administrative efforts. This simple shift in thinking will allow you to fully use your assistant as a member of your team.

THE THREE-STEP MODEL TO INCREASE YOUR ASSISTANT'S ROLE IN MARKETING

1. DECIDE WHAT ADDED ROLE(S) YOU WANT YOUR ASSISTANT TO PLAY. Do you want assistance with market research, scheduling meetings, and tracking down information needed to make decisions about CLE or industry conferences to attend? Do you need someone to take care of your expense reports, coordinate clients and colleagues across multiple time zones, and ensure that you're staying in regular contact with clients, even when they don't have active matters with you? Decide exactly what you want this new partnership to include and write that down. Dream big.

2. SET UP A MEETING WITH YOUR ASSISTANT TO EXPLAIN YOUR VISION. Schedule a separate meeting for this conversation, rather than including it at the end of your daily conversation. Ideally, take your assistant to coffee or lunch outside of the office. You want to highlight the importance of the issue. Bring your notes from Step 1 and explain your thoughts on this proposed new partnership. Ask for comments. Then be silent and listen very carefully for what comes next. You are likely to get a strong positive response.

Your assistant wants interesting and challenging work every bit as much as you do. Just as importantly, she wants to be a part of something that is important and meaningful. A partnership with you is very unusual and a nice expansion of interesting work beyond the day-to-day matters you typically provide. You may also be surprised that an assistant who works for three or four attorneys can suddenly find time to manage these new activities. The power of interesting and meaningful work cannot be overstated.

3. ASK YOUR ASSISTANT FOR IDEAS ON HOW TO IMPLEMENT YOUR VISION. Notice that Step 1 asked you to define the scope of the relationship. It did not ask you to decide how to make that happen. Employ the "ASK don't TELL" approach we use in our coaching program and ask your assistant whether it interests him

or her. Ask for input on how to make the vision a reality. It's highly unlikely that you're the best person to design how to execute the tasks you want done. Let the expert design the system.

If you want your expense reports handled by your assistant, explain the firm's policy and ask for advice on how to manage it so that you no longer have a pile of receipts from trips stuffed in an envelope in your desk. If you need a better follow-up system for your speaking engagements, explain the action steps involved and then ask for assistance setting up a system to make the follow-up happen smoothly and without a lot of time and effort on your part.

If you're happy when your assistant simply shows up for work on time and has a civil word or two, then sharing this model may not work for you. In those cases, you might see whether some other person in your firm is willing to take on this new role.

If you're wondering where you will find the time to implement this three-step model, it all boils down to priorities and motivation. It simply won't happen if you never make the time to try. The secret to your success in developing a team relationship with your assistant rests on your ability to shift your thinking and on your ability to execute around your priorities. These are the same skills that are critical to successful business development.

As a final incentive for those still on the fence about forming a partnership with an assistant, consider this: If a professional works approximately 2,400 hours a year (including billable, non-billable, firm administration, professional development, and other items) and can shift just 5 percent of that time to an assistant, 120 hours a year become available for other things. Better still, most of the tasks you shift to your assistant will be completed faster and better than when you attempt them! You also gain time to focus on things you enjoy more and activities that are a better use of your education and experience. Not a bad tradeoff for an investment of a couple of hours of time and a cup of coffee or a lunch.

PART V

Improving
Relationships
Within Your Firm

Internal marketing is a neglected but fruitful area for directing your business development energy.

33

RAISING YOUR INTERNAL PROFILE

How Can I Network Within My Firm?

We have been asked this question many times during coaching sessions: "How can I raise my internal profile?" The best way to raise your profile within the firm is to genuinely care about the people in your firm. Don't just give lip service to the fact that you care, demonstrate it! Do a favor for someone inside the firm each day. These favors can extend to staff members such as your assistant, chief marketing officer, or chief operating officer.

How to Raise Your Internal Profile

If you eat lunch at your desk every day, you're not likely to raise your internal profile very much. On the bright side, if you eat lunch at your desk every day, you've got nowhere to go but up. It won't take much to raise your profile. Here are some ideas to stimulate your thinking:

1. Give yourself a quota for making internal connections. We define networking as putting people together for *their* mutual benefit. If, on a daily basis, you introduce your partner, associate, or staff member to someone he or she will benefit

from meeting, you are off to a great start. How many of you commuted to work this morning thinking about which person in the firm you would like to help today? One internal connection per day could put you in the top tier of your firm in a year.

Connect at the point where you have mutual interests and passions. One of our clients was a litigator who loved gardening. She learned from her CMO that another partner on the corporate side had won an award for his gardening prowess. She called him to introduce herself and to find out more. Not only was a connection made, but a relationship was born. As she commented, the chances of him contacting her if a litigation issue arises went up dramatically as a result of that connection.

2. Take a rainmaker to breakfast or lunch. This is an important subset of the previous idea. A young partner with one of our Canadian clients realized there were at least 30 people in his office he could approach to learn how they became top rainmakers. What follows are some suggested questions.

- How did you develop your network?

- How did you meet your key referral sources?

- How do you find the time to do it all?

- How long did it take to generate $1 million in business?

- If you had to start over again today, how many years do you think it would take?

- What system do you use to generate the business?

- How much work do you generate each year outside your practice area?

This same partner initially resisted the idea of approaching colleagues in other geographical offices, until his coach asked how long it would take him to meet with the 30 partners from his city. He concluded it might be a year. So he was asked, "And then what?" He had two choices: Start over again with those same 30 people or make a point of reaching out to other partners. For example, he could contact those who were not in his city just prior to the firm's annual retreat and schedule some time with them. He liked that idea.

He could also ask partners based locally whom they knew well from the other offices. That way it wouldn't feel like making a cold call. That hadn't occurred to him either. It takes persistence to secure meetings with your firm's top rainmakers. Rainmakers are usually very busy people. Persistence with them will serve as great practice for when you seek meetings with successful people and senior executives outside the firm.

3. ORGANIZE A VALUABLE FORUM FEATURING YOUR RAINMAKERS. One of our clients created a forum within her firm wherein female rainmakers shared their insights and successes with other female professionals. It was extremely well received. If you want to raise your profile, take on the task of organizing a comparable forum in your firm.

4. MAKE MORE OUT OF YOUR ANNUAL MEETINGS AND RETREATS. Very few of our clients consider their annual meetings or retreats as opportunities to raise their profiles. Give yourself a quota for the number of meaningful connections you plan on making at your annual meeting. In addition, make a handful of follow-up calls to partners after the annual meeting is over. If you have a far-flung network of offices, this is the chance to spend face time with people you rarely see. Imagine if you asked ten partners you barely know: "How will I know when I am talking to your ideal client?"

5. ADOPT A "HOW CAN I HELP?" MINDSET. A new partner within a large New York City firm was relaying to his coach how he made partner by going the extra mile. However, he was having a tough time gaining traction as a partner and couldn't pinpoint why. It turns out that he had subconsciously reverted to thinking "how can others help me" once he made partner. His coach was astonished to learn that he had stopped doing what got him there! Once he became aware of what he had done, he reverted back to his previous formula. He loves helping others and has returned to doing just that as a way to raise his profile.

Another client of ours was very systematic about helping others. In his state, OSHA posts a list each Wednesday of employers that could be cited. On Thursday, OSHA holds hearings to decide whether the companies will be cited. Each Wednesday, he pores over that list. If he sees a client of the firm on that list, he has his assistant identify who the billing partner is for that client. He calls his partner, tells her the situation, and leaves it up to her to alert her client. Nine times out of ten he helps his partner look like a hero in the eyes of her client.

This same lawyer monitors a court reporting service of new filings for the same purpose. He used the same system to alert his partners to opportunities outside his specialty. In one case, his efforts allowed his partner to call the CEO of a company that was being sued on a products liability claim. Needless to say, his reputation within the products liability group is very favorable.

6. SHARE KUDOS AND CREDIT FOR SUCCESS LIBERALLY. In particular, share billing credits generously. One of our clients had a strong desire to increase the size of his practice to rainmaker proportions. However, when we began our work together, he had a gloomy view of many of his partners outside his practice area. This was based on how inattentive they were to the clients and work he brought them on the rare occasions when he generated new work. The solution for him was counterintuitive: share billing credits. He was amazed at the turnaround this prompted. His profile and his book of business is *much* higher today, and the quality of the clients he is serving has increased, too.

Ninety percent of the people in any organization spend far too much time looking out for themselves. If you really want to stand out in your firm, be among the 10 percent who find purpose and joy in helping others.

Can you imagine working in a firm where everyone did these things? You can't control whether your partners do these things, but you can control whether or not *you* do them. Get started today! Who knows, maybe you'll rub off on the others and it will become a firm where everyone does these things.

Of this you can be sure: If you generate $5 million in new business, but only $1 million of it is in your practice area, you will become *very* well known in other areas of the firm.

Approach every conversation with your partners and referral sources as a chance to deepen the relationship.

┌─────┐
│ 34 │
└─────┘

QUESTIONS TO HELP YOU CONNECT WITH PARTNERS

What Can I Ask to Deepen My Relationships with Partners?

Most professionals want to know how to make cross-selling more prevalent within their firms. There is often a palpable sense of urgency because there is so much opportunity. It's even more pronounced with lateral hires who come aboard hoping for great synergies in their new firms.

Don't sit in your office hoping someone will drop by or call. Instead, get out among your partners! Have more conversations, and make sure *none* of them is random or perfunctory. Common sense suggests you won't secure many introductions if you don't have a significant relationship with others.

The root cause of this dearth of connections is a lack of imagination and knowing how to do it. If you're not happy with the number of introductions made, you can single-handedly change that by having more high-energy conversations. In case you can't think of any high-energy questions, several follow to get you started. Try one or more of them the next time you are having a cup of coffee with one of your partners.

And for goodness sake, expand the pool of people you meet with on a regular basis. Stop having lunch with the usual suspects. Remember that the goal with all of these questions is to build greater rapport.

1. *To which groups have you spoken recently?* If you really want to get your partner fired up about you, ask *him* for a copy of the last taped presentation he gave! This lets you preview your partner's presentation skills, and lets you learn more about his substantive knowledge and what value he might add to your clients' businesses.

2. *How did you get your first major client?* Most people remember how they got their first client and asking about it allows them to relive their glorious success.

3. *What was the toughest client you've ever brought in?*

4. *How do you deal with high-maintenance clients?*

5. *What was the most satisfying client you have ever landed?*

6. *What have you found most satisfying about your work in the past month?*

7. *What have you found works best in attracting new clients?* This question allows you to learn everyone's secrets, including the firm's best rainmakers. Armed with this information, you can streamline your own efforts.

8. *What do you wish someone had taught you from your first day on the job?*

9. *What did you learn from your mentor about keeping great clients?*

10. *Who is the greatest person you've ever worked with, and what made her great?*

11. *What industries do you know the best? Where did you learn so much about them?*

12. *What single anecdote best summarizes your approach to marketing?*

13. *Which of the clients do you feel the greatest connection with? Why?*

14. *What is the most enjoyable and fun part of your work?*

15. *Which partners within the firm send you the best clients?*

16. *What kinds of work allow you to express your unique talents?*

17. *Where do you feel you are underappreciated?*

18. *What is your favorite hobby?*

19. *What passions do you have outside of work?*

20. *If you didn't have your current job, what kinds of things would you do instead?*

21. *How did you land your celebrity client?*

This is by no means an exhaustive list. Let your imagination run wild. One caveat: Don't ask all of these questions in a single sitting; rather, put most of these questions to the same person during the course of a year. It might take several years to get through them all, but it will deepen the relationship like nothing you've ever done. Those who think these questions are too artificial will be hampered by that belief. One of the reasons why so little cross-selling happens is the frequency of meaningless or perfunctory conversations held among the people in your firm. You can have several dozen nearly meaningless conversations with your partners in a year and accomplish almost nothing *or* you can have one or two enlightening conversations per week with each of them. The choice is yours.

When speaking internally, energize your audience
to the point of taking action.

35

INTERNAL PRESENTATIONS TO YOUR PARTNERS

HOW DO I OBTAIN MORE WORK AND NEW CLIENTS FROM MY PARTNERS?

If approached correctly, internal speaking presentations present similar or greater opportunities than those from external public speaking. Many professionals make the same mistakes speaking internally as they do when speaking outside the firm. Foremost among them is doing little or no meaningful preparation. Most assume the primary purpose of an internal presentation is to educate the audience about the speaker and his or her practice. When speaking internally, it's important to go well beyond telling your partners what you do. The purpose is to energize your audience to the point of taking action! In most cases, the objective is to make your telephone ring. You want at least one or more of your partners to visit you or call you after the presentation to talk about a client who came to mind during your presentation. How you prepare for and conduct the presentation can heavily influence that outcome. Here are several keys to successful internal presentations.

1. MAKE YOUR PARTNERS LOOK GOOD. You aren't there to impress them with what you know. Since they're spending their time listening to your presentation, you should be thinking about "what's in it for them." Your job is to show them how you can make them look good to their clients. One securities litigator took this idea to heart before speaking to her corporate partners. Instead of telling them what she did, she explained how she was going to make them look good by helping their clients. This approach generated multiple phone calls immediately after the presentation, and, in several cases, she secured meetings with her partners' clients.

2. START YOUR PRESENTATION WITH A GREAT QUESTION TO STIMULATE DIALOGUE WITH YOUR PARTNERS. Suppose you are a bankruptcy lawyer speaking to the corporate group. You could begin your presentation by asking whether anyone in the audience has a client who is struggling financially. If so, you could ask whether he knew there are things he could do to help his client avoid bankruptcy. Or perhaps you could ask whether your partners have any clients who are no longer paying their bills promptly after many years of routinely making prompt payment. This could be a sign that a client's business is experiencing distress.

Or consider another example: While conducting a retreat for the tax department of a large law firm, I asked the group to come up with ideas on how to make their non-tax partners look good. They came up with the idea of showing litigators how to make their clients' structured settlements tax deductible. Two questions you might use when speaking to litigators are: "Are you really close to settling a dispute with the other side, but can't quite get your client or the other side to go along?" and "Are you concerned about having to send a large bill to a client on a case you just settled?" In either situation, if the answer is yes, he or she may be very interested in learning how your tax expertise can make the settlement possible or make the large bill more palatable.

3. CALL SEVERAL PARTNERS BEFORE YOU SPEAK. You want to call a handful of partners in advance of your talk for two reasons.

Their input will help you customize your presentation, and such a call helps you build relationships with your partners. For example, the lateral partner within one firm was not happy with the paucity of introductions he received from his partners. He had spoken inside the firm a handful of times, but had not enjoyed great results from those presentations. Use your internal presentation as a basis for reaching otherwise unreachable partners. Even if they don't attend your presentation, you've spent face time with them building the relationship. If it's done well, you don't care whether they attend your presentation.

This also gives you a great reason to call your partners before the talk and solicit ideas on what other partners in the practice group might want to hear. One lateral had been at her firm for two years and admitted she didn't know many partners and even fewer rainmakers. She agreed that, if she had followed this practice from the day she arrived, she'd be much better known throughout the firm. This is the perfect chance to have a high-energy conversation.

4. MAKE BROWN-BAG LUNCHES MEMORABLE. Some firms sponsor periodic lunches where a partner or a practice group is featured during lunch. These lunches usually fizzle because the firm doesn't hold the presenting professionals accountable for making the presentation interesting. Making it a requirement that each speaker interview at least five professionals in the firm before giving the presentation could improve the success of the lunches, make them more memorable, and facilitate the building of relationships within the firm.

5. OFFER A GIVEAWAY TO YOUR PARTNERS. Consider offering your partners a list of questions they can ask clients about your area, since they often won't know what questions to ask. It also gives them an excuse to contact you after your presentation.

6. FOLLOW UP WITH MEMBERS OF THE AUDIENCE. While it would be wonderful if your partners took the bait and called you, many of them won't because of everyday pressures of their

practices. So take the initiative and call or visit them. When you do, be sure to have some questions prepared to direct the conversation, such as:

- Did the presentation cover all the issues you wanted me to cover? If not, this is an excellent opportunity to follow up with more dialogue.

- As a result of the presentation, did you think of any clients who might benefit from knowing about, or knowing more about, the subject? Obviously, if the answer is yes, then you'll want to follow up to see whether your partner is willing to set up a meeting between you and that client. You could make it clear to your partner that the initial meeting will be at no charge to the client to make him or her more willing to set up the meeting.

- As a result of the presentation, are there other topics you would like me to cover?

- Is there anything I could have done differently to make the presentation more useful to you or to your clients?

The list is endless, but it illustrates the need to prepare for the call.

7. FINALLY, ASK FOR A CLEARLY DEFINED COMMITMENT FROM YOUR PARTNER. When you contact a partner after the presentation, be prepared to ask for a follow-up action. If the presentation or conversation stimulates that partner's thoughts about a particular client, then you can ask him or her to set up a meeting with the client at a particular time to discuss how you can be of service to the client. One intellectual property lawyer seeking an introduction approached a litigator and firm rainmaker with three options in mind: (1) a three-way meeting, (2) a three-way conference call, or (3) a letter prepared for the litigator's signature that would go to the client. His partner agreed to the third option and a meeting between the two of them to discuss it.

Remember, the purpose of internal presentations is to develop relationships within the firm that can lead to work with existing clients, and perhaps new clients. Don't waste your time making presentations if you're going to approach them haphazardly.

Every day thousands of professionals make internal presentations and completely miss golden opportunities. Refer to this chapter when preparing for your next internal presentation, or give it to a partner who's scheduled to give one, for ideas on how to make the most of this radically underutilized marketing tool.

Great coaches can see greatness in you that you can't see in yourself.

36

TOP TEN COACHING ERRORS TO AVOID

How Can Coaching Skills Be Applied to Our Conversations with Colleagues?

More and more firms and businesses are adopting a coaching methodology to their professional development efforts. Senior professionals and marketing and business development staff persons are working with coaches and, in the process, learning coaching techniques to help develop their colleagues. While we applaud this movement, we have noted that some skills get lost between the learning and the application of new-found coaching skills.

What follows are what we believe are the top ten coaching errors professionals make when they try to apply coaching skills to their conversations with colleagues. We have also included our recommendations on how to remediate these errors.

1. TELLING INSTEAD OF ASKING. It is okay to give advice when you are coaching. However, it is not okay to simply tell someone what to do. Questions are powerful tools. They can plant seeds, inspire action, shift perspectives, and challenge beliefs. All of

151

these changes occur far more easily when one is asking open-ended questions that elicit responses, rather than telling someone what to do.

2. FORCING "MY WAY OR THE HIGHWAY." Coaching is about getting the best out of another person. It is *not* about telling another professional how to behave or asking him to shape his behavior to match the coach's. What works for you might not work for your colleagues. Help them discover their unique approaches. Don't force them to adopt yours.

3. NOT WALKING YOUR TALK. A good coach models appropriate behavior. Lots of people are good at talking about what someone else needs to do but are not good at modeling that behavior themselves. Demonstrate the behaviors that you find important. Your credibility is based on what you do, not on what you say.

4. TALKING FIRST, RATHER THAN LISTENING. "First seek to understand, then to be understood."[1] It is impossible to get someone to see your point of view without making an effort to understand her point of view. Talking first instead of listening is a great way to communicate that your view is the most important view, but it is not a method that is conducive to getting the best out of another person.

5. FOCUSING ON TOO MANY THINGS AT ONE TIME. Most people focus on far too many goals when they seek to change their behavior. Typically, people can successfully work on only one or two behaviors at a time. So instead of pointing out all the issues you have with your colleague, limit your focus by choosing the one or two items that will have the biggest impact on improving his success.

6. IMPOSING A VISION ON ANOTHER PERSON. We have all come across someone who reminds us of a younger version of ourselves. If we are really honest, we may even admit that this young associate is even better than we were at that age. Our biggest challenge is to give that associate the room to grow into whatever it is that *she* wants to be — not what *we* want her to become.

7. FORGETTING TO TAKE YOUR OWN MEDICINE. One of the best ways to model appropriate coaching behavior is to be both the coach and the client. Your subordinates often have much to teach you. Demonstrate powerful coaching skills by being a continuous learner who learns from anyone and everyone. There are few forces more powerful in convincing people to change their lives than witnessing you changing your own.

8. WAITING TOO LONG. The best time to make a point is immediately after encountering a behavior that you would like to see changed. For example, if a colleague does not follow up with someone to whom he gave advice at the end of a speech, ask him about it the same week. Don't wait for a month to go by before you inquire about how the follow-up went.

9. FORGETTING TO FOLLOW UP. Similarly, make sure you consistently follow up with your colleagues. It is a powerful way to build credibility. When you follow up with people, you demonstrate that you care about them. That is a powerful force with which to motivate people to achieve their best. This also demonstrates that you take the coaching, and the person, seriously.

10. PRETENDING THAT YOU HAVE ALL THE ANSWERS. Coaching is not consulting, practicing law, or conducting business! You don't need to have all the answers to be successful as a coach, and indeed you probably won't have them all. Instead, it is often more important to have the right questions. Let go of your need to be right, your need to be the expert, and your need to persuade someone else. Let go, and let your colleague grow!

Learning coaching techniques and applying them to situations with your colleagues require thought and effort. To provide helpful coaching moments, give some of these recommendations a try. You'll find that applying your new-found coaching skills can be rewarding when you're focused on staying in service to the person you are trying to coach.

If you want to see service levels increase dramatically on work you originate and your partners handle, start volunteering to split billing credit.

37

VOLUNTEERING TO SPLIT BILLING CREDIT

How Can We Encourage Collaboration, Improve Service, Inspire Associates, and Free Senior Partners to Market More?

Splitting billing credit is still not very popular among professional services firms. But correctly applied, it can increase collaboration from partners, improve service to clients, inspire associates to work harder, and free senior professionals to spend their time rainmaking.

One of our clients experienced success on a number of levels. He got so much better at landing new work that he couldn't handle it all by himself. This required him to hand off more work to others in the firm. However, he became increasingly frustrated by his partners' lack of responsiveness to clients he brought in the door. His coach offered a solution that he didn't like when he first heard it: Offer to split billing credit. He operated in a firm that didn't make a habit of splitting the billing credit, and billing credit was used to determine bonus compensation. Nevertheless, he began to offer to split the billing credit and noticed an immediate and striking improvement in responsiveness at all levels of the firm. He has seen a dramatic increase in partner responsiveness to his requests for help. Before he adopted this practice, he complained that partners were unwilling to serve his clients as they did their own. Splitting billing credit solved that problem.

On the rare occasions when the partner with whom he split billing credit wasn't able to satisfy the client, he went back to his partner and asked, "What's fair?" Never once has he been disappointed with their suggestions for reapportioning credit. The partner who had stopped doing work on the matter agreed that it made no sense to receive any billing credit.

Once he began splitting billing credit, this client noticed that it had several effects on his life. First, partners and the associates they supervised delivered higher levels of service to his clients. Second, he was able to take a two-week vacation without spending a big chunk of it on the phone or sending e-mails. Third, he noticed more partners in the firm were beginning to seek out his opinions. He also began receiving better treatment from people within the firm and was accorded more respect. Finally, he focused more on managing client relationships, rather than simply doing the work. He also discovered another wonderful thing — bringing in work that others can service doesn't eat up as much of his time. He has a very busy practice and doesn't want a lot of new work for himself. He can be much choosier about the type of work he does and brings into the firm. He also has greater control of his own destiny. Oh, and one more important thing — he is having more fun!

If you want your firm's top line to increase by $3 million or more, put your best rainmakers through an extended top-tier coaching program.

38

THE PERILS OF INSECURE RAINMAKERS

How Could Some of Our Top Rainmakers Double Their Books of Business?

In working with professionals, our coaches see all kinds of dysfunctional behavior. Perhaps the behavior most often tolerated is the insecure rainmaker. Every firm has at least one rainmaker (and sometimes several) who is not the least bit interested in having other partners around her achieve parity as rainmakers. These elitist rainmakers enjoy the rarefied air of being among the top producers in their firms. That's because they have more power when they produce a book of business that is bigger than most people within the firm. According to Cleat Simmons, general counsel of SunGard Higher Education Managed Services, "Power is allocated to partners within firms based on rank and dollar production." The thinking goes something like this: "If I'm the only one in my firm who has a $5 million book of business, my power base is bigger than if there are two or three people who produce those numbers."

Insecure Rainmakers Hurt Your Firm

Insecure rainmakers hurt your firm in two primary ways: (1) They don't produce as much business as they could and (2) They don't allow others to equal or surpass them because they feel threatened by others. This leads to them *not* taking a hands-on development role. As another rainmaker put it, "It undermines teamwork and team building." We believe a fair number of firms with too many insecure rainmakers will become extinct in the next five to ten years.

Insecure rainmakers are the biggest underperforming asset in most firms. It's our experience that some of the top producers are the biggest underperformers. You read it right: *Some of the top producers are the biggest underperformers.* Here's why: In most firms, the individual who has a $2 million book of business is held in high regard. This is true even if he inherited that business from a retired partner. No one bothers to ask whether that partner is capable of generating $4 **million** in business. From a purely economic point of view, who is the bigger underperformer? The partner who has a $400,000 book of business who could get to $750,000 with some help or the partner who has a $2 million book but could be doing $3 million or $4 million. The answer is obvious.

Many firms have top producers with sizable books of business who are held up as models for others to emulate. However, when you peek under the hood, you realize that these people are all too often resting on their laurels. Instead of generating business, they are merely minding existing business. The truth is, these individuals could easily *double* or *triple* their books of business with some focused coaching and a little healthy competition. In effect, some of your top producers are cruising!

Recognizing the Insecure Rainmaker

Insecurities in rainmakers can manifest themselves in several ways: They don't invite others along on business development meetings, they don't coach people to greater success, they don't pursue work collaboratively, they don't share speaking leads they don't want or shouldn't take, and they don't provide third-party training and coaching to partners who want it. They are also a potential liability risk to the firm because they often work hard, handling matters they ae not proficient in, rather than having the firm's real experts deal with the issues.

They may give lots of lip service to developing people and to teamwork, but their behavior tells a different tale. They don't do anything to encourage, or even allow, people in the firm who are below them in business generation to improve because these others might achieve parity. If their power base is strong enough, they may even sabotage efforts to institute business development training programs for others in the firm.

Another form of insecurity our coaches see is in partners competing against each other for the same client. Each is more interested in getting to the client first and getting the billing or origination credit than in ensuring the firm's success in getting the client, regardless of the billing or origination credit.

INSECURE RAINMAKER OR ABUNDANT RAINMAKER?

How can you tell whether your rainmakers are insecure or whether they operate from an abundance mentality? The ones who are truly secure do their best to help others increase their books of business, while the insecure ones don't lift a finger to help others unless it's in their own personal best interest. The secure ones are vocal advocates for getting their partners the training needed to get to the next level, while the insecure ones are detractors. Tolerating insecure rainmakers can lead to top producers and firm leaders leaving to start their own firms or go in-house.

What's the solution? Challenge your rainmakers! Then see how many respond to the challenge.

Try this challenge: Ask six to ten of your best rainmakers to participate in an 18- to 24-month program in which they work with a top-flight coach. They are only allowed to participate if they are prepared to commit to increase their books of business by $500,000 over the previous year's books of business. If you put six rainmakers through this program and they all achieve their objectives, it will yield $3 million in *increased* revenue to your firm. If you put ten rainmakers through this program and they all achieve their objectives, it will yield $5 million in *increased* revenue to your firm.

Any takers? Please let us know if you decide to accept the challenge. This is a very simple program to implement. It is also one that will provide an enormous return on your firm's most costly investment: its people.

Your partners won't do things for your reasons; they will only do things for their reasons. Invest the time needed to find out what will prompt them to action.

39

GETTING UNRESPONSIVE PARTNERS TO MARKET!

HOW CAN WE MOTIVATE PARTNERS TO COOPERATE IN MARKETING?

We are sometimes asked how to best deal with a partner who will not respond to another partner's voicemail and e-mail requests to help land a new business opportunity. Often these unresponsive partners are great service partners, but won't respond to calls for help in the pursuit of new business. This is a source of frustration for the more marketing-minded partners. These resisters are often accused of not being team players. Sometimes the solution is very simple: Visiting them in person is a much stronger way to build connections. If you visit someone and you still don't get the response you want, perhaps it would help to have the person work with a coach.

WHY IS YOUR PARTNER RESISTING?

You are more likely to gain someone's cooperation if you understand what he's thinking. The next time someone resists, try something new. Either you or a firm manager could pay a visit to your partner with a clear goal of learning the underlying cause for his lack of response. Too often we assume the person lacks motivation. That may be true, but there is only one way to find out — and that's to ask the unresponsive partner.

During the meeting, ask him: "How responsive do you think you are perceived to be by your fellow partners when it comes to helping bring new business into the firm?" (Notice that you are asking him to rate himself.) Your goal isn't to judge or put him on the defensive, but to understand his thinking. Once an answer is out on the table, you might learn he simply makes getting new business a very low priority. If that's the case, you might say: "We'd like you to be more responsive. Is there anything we can do to help you become more so?" If his answer is "Nothing," then you have a problem. More often, his answer won't be that gloomy. In effect, what this conversation will yield are the reasons why your partner wants to be on the team. Armed with those reasons, try to secure his cooperation.

If you're uncomfortable with the direct approach, try an indirect one. This presumes there is more than one unresponsive partner in your firm. For example, suppose there are three unresponsive partners within your firm. You can ask Partner A, "I need your help on something. How do I get B or C to respond to new business opportunities?" In addition, you can ask B, "How do I get A and C to respond?" Finally, you can ask C a similar question, "How do I get A and B to respond?"

You will often hear an autobiographical response to your question from each of them. You can then use this information to probe deeper into the reasons why each partner is unresponsive. Will this work every time? No, but it's far more effective than accusing them of being unresponsive or lacking team-player attitudes. Again, these conversations should yield the reasons why your partners want to be on the team.

GETTING PARTNERS TO DEVOTE TIME FOR MARKETING

Another skill that's rarely discussed is helping your partners to devote meaningful amounts of time learning prospects' business during the relationship-building phase. Obviously, this time will not be billable. Your firm's best rainmakers have a gift for enrolling others in doing this, while the rest of us marvel at their talent. The best way to get *others* to do work up-front for free before your firm is hired is for *you* to model that same behavior. How many hours have *you* "donated" to helping others land a major project? If others see your requests as a one-way street, you can forget about securing cooperation. The next time you are irked because someone won't pitch in, be sure to look in the mirror first. Maybe others are treating you the exact same way you treat them.

Keep your communication with partners short and direct. If you want help, ask for it in person whenever possible. If you must use e-mail, state your request for help in the subject line or first sentence or two of an e-mail.

It rarely helps to label your partners "slugs," "unmotivated," or similar pejorative labels. No one likes being labeled or condemned. Becoming a great rainmaker requires securing help from the people around you, particularly the unmotivated ones, because they are a rarely utilized resource. If you don't get their help, you'd better resign yourself to landing smaller deals and having a much smaller book of business.

Take an associate to a business development meeting today.

40

DEVELOPING THE NEXT GENERATION OF RAINMAKERS

HOW CAN WE CLOSE THE GAP BETWEEN TODAY'S AND TOMORROW'S RAINMAKERS?

Many firms are facing a growing problem. There is an enormous gap between a firm's existing rainmakers and the crop of people who will be expected to keep the firm going and growing in the next decade. In some firms, 80 percent of the firm's rainmaking capacity resides with fewer than 20 percent of its partners. And those partners are in their late fifties and early sixties. Here are several things your firm can do to start closing the gap.

START ASSOCIATES ON RELATIONSHIP BUILDING EARLIER

Too many firms wait too long to teach rainmaking skills to their junior people. Maraia & Associates, Inc., performed a study in 2005 that asked, "When is the best time to get your professionals started on business development?" The consensus was: In their third or fourth year. Consider the fourth-year associate who has plenty of contacts at her peer level who would become decision-makers in the coming decade. By remaining sequestered in her office just billing hours, she won't invest the time needed to cultivate these relationships. Starting associates earlier doesn't mean pressuring them to bring in business. Rather, it makes sense for them to intentionally cultivate their networks now, so when they are expected to be rainmakers, they will be better able to do so.

By not starting earlier, associates will be handicapped once they reach the partner ranks. A shocking number of new partners have totally lost touch with their peers from college or post-graduate school and prior work venues. They find it very awkward to start calling on their peers once they make partner without looking like an opportunist.

Teach and Delegate Meeting Preparation to Associates

Do associates know exactly how to prepare for a meeting with a prospective client or how to use speaking to expand their networks? Most junior people would answer these questions with a resounding no. Our programs are in high demand because we give junior and senior people a framework for *how* to do these things.

One rainmaker spent 25 hours preparing for a meeting with a highly desirable client. While debriefing with his coach, he realized he could have delegated a hefty portion of that preparation to members of his team who also attended the meeting. It is never too early to teach people good preparation habits. In our workshops, we ask people whether they understand the importance of preparing for a meeting with a prospective client. We follow up by asking, "How many go into meetings with prospective clients prepared 100 percent of the time?" Usually very few people raise their hands.

Bring Associates to Marketing Meetings

Have your best rainmakers bring others from your firm to their marketing meetings. There is considerable value in letting your next generation of professionals see a variety of your best people in action. Where it's appropriate, have your junior people prepare several questions for the meeting.

In addition, give your less experienced marketers a *meaningful* role in meetings with prospects and during client pitches. Clients are very sophisticated and will *not* appreciate it — nor will they be impressed — when you bring a team of five individuals but they only hear from one or two senior people. Let your junior people participate in proportion to the amount of work they will do for the client. If your junior people will be doing 80 percent of the work, let them conduct 60 to 80 percent of the meeting. Don't think so much about what you want them to say; rather, coach them to develop thoughtful questions to ask your prospective client. Also coach them to listen carefully to the client's answers.

HELP THEM DEFINE THEIR IDEAL CLIENT

Promote answers to the question, "How would you describe your ideal client?" This is a great idea for both senior and junior people. Once they articulate a specific answer, ask, "How many people do you know who meet those criteria who are *not* your clients?" The answer we hear most often is "less than a handful." These questions help younger or newer professionals focus on what's needed to build their networks intentionally and with a purpose. And the more specific the answers, the better. For example, if someone says "a large corporate client," push the person to define what that means. After some coaching, she might respond with something like "a computer hardware company that has a dozen or more U.S. manufacturing sites that have an environmental waste stream disposal issue."

START SHARING BILLING CREDIT

One of our clients hit a ceiling on the size of his practice until he started offering to share billing credit with his partners. His practice, which had been stuck at $500,000 per year, ballooned to several million dollars, all because he began to share the credit.

LET YOUR NEXT GENERATION WORK WITH A COACH

More firms are starting to add people who can coach others to their marketing staffs. Top-quality coaches are not easy to find, but it's worth hiring them when you find them. One CMO was so hot on the idea that she was willing to pay a highly talented coach a salary that exceeded her own. Great coaching accelerates skill development in ways that are hard to fathom. It's been our experience that young professionals can develop skills five to ten times faster working closely with an effective coach, rather than going about it in an ad hoc manner or through trial and error.

Do yourself and your firm a great service and start developing your next generation of rainmakers *today*.

Make someone else's success a subject of your concern today.

41

CREATING A RAINMAKER

HOW CAN I MENTOR AN ASSOCIATE AND HELP MY PRACTICE GROW?

It is always nice to share stories about clients who are inspired about growing their practices. One such rainmaker and long-time client began thinking about mentoring young lawyers after reading an issue of *The Maraia Minutes*. Upon reading the article, he immediately thought of a young associate he could help. This associate was in his second year of practice and was very gung ho about learning this rainmaker's area of practice, OSHA regulation. This rainmaker's firm is based in a state that borders Mexico. The young associate was Hispanic and fluent in Spanish.

Known nationally, the rainmaker spoke frequently to management on OSHA issues but he had become frustrated through the years at needing a translator for the Spanish-speaking segment of his client base. He wondered if his associate might become well-known in the Hispanic community speaking about OSHA issues. The rainmaker approached his associate and told him what he was thinking. The associate was both thrilled and nervous. Most importantly, he was on board with the idea and appreciative of his mentor's willingness to further his career. The rainmaker's thinking wasn't entirely altruistic, because if his associate succeeded it would give them a track to developing more business and further strengthen existing client relationships.

This rainmaker started calling influential members of his network and asked if they wanted his associate to give similar presentations completely in Spanish. The members of his network, including those from the Hispanic community, *loved* his idea and the fact that he was willing to help his young associate in this way. *He also learned that there was a huge market that was being ignored.*

Great rainmakers don't hesitate to help others, and we commend this rainmaker for making the effort on his associate's behalf. We hope this rainmaker's efforts on behalf of his associate inspires *you* to do something equally simple yet brilliant. Who knows how many will benefit from your taking someone under your wing?

Overloading your best associates with too much work is perceived by them, in most cases, as a form of punishment.

42

STOP PUNISHING YOUR BEST ASSOCIATES!

How Can You Avoid Associate Churn?

Every firm in the world has associates who are so valuable they would like to clone more of them. We've noticed in our work that many firms unwittingly do things that punish their best associates. That's right. They *punish their best people.* Not only that, but firms actually reward their worst performers for their inability to learn quickly. How can that be?

Consider this hypothetical example: You have a fifth-year associate in the employee benefits area who has always been a superstar. Every partner in your firm loves delegating assignments to her because all she needs to do is "breathe fumes from the file" and she delivers her finished work product on time and done exceptionally well. Moreover, clients rave about her and she is great at bringing along more junior associates. The simple fact is, these people are performing like your best young partners. You wonder to yourself why the firm can't find more associates like her. The only problem is that these kinds of associates are in very short supply.

The more typical associate requires two to ten times more of *your* valuable time getting up-to-speed and often his work is not as thorough or accurate. Faced with the simple choice of giving work to your superstar or giving work to your less-capable performers, what will you do? Most will keep giving assignments to the top performers. Sometimes we even treat people as if they are machines that don't tire of the workload. That's a big mistake. The reward to your worst performers comes in the form of fewer assignments.

You may be unintentionally driving out your firm's best associates. The reason you (and every partner in the firm) like this associate is obvious. It takes you less time and energy to bring her up-to-speed. If you don't have to do lots of rework, it saves you even more time. If such associates are in a pool with others, they'll receive a larger share of work. They'll always be in demand and bill more hours than the rest of your associates. That makes them more profitable, too!

So what's the problem? By overloading the best associates, you're actually *punishing* them. Look at it from your top associate's perspective. She gets more assignments than anyone else in the pool and is rewarded with the small bonuses or other incentives that you give top-performing associates. Would you give up your time at home with your family, or whatever you enjoy doing with your free time, for the extra $X dollars that you're being paid?

Think about it this way. Many firms reward their top producers (in terms of hours) with bonuses for the extra hours. If you're paying an associate $10,000 for the last 1,000 hours she worked, it amounts to $10 per hour. Does anyone think a good lawyer's time is worth only $10 per hour.

Instead of punishing your best associates, think of your underperforming associates as a hidden resource. If you take the time to properly delegate work to them and they get up-to-speed, you have other performers who initially weren't stars but have become late bloomers. You'll get the same benefits from doing this as you get from overworking your top people.

Whether or not they become late bloomers is almost entirely within your control. Yes, it does take more time with late bloomers, *but* unless you're at the top of the pecking order in your firm, having access to the overachievers may not be an option anyway.

There is contributing factor to this problem. Your partners are very poor at delegating work. Most simply don't know how to delegate effectively. We know this from personal experience in our coaching work with all kinds of professionals. Many, perhaps most, partners have the unrealistic belief that superstar associates should be the norm. But for every superstar associate, another five or ten associates need to be brought along more slowly. You can shorten the time it takes to get an average associate up-to-speed three to twenty times faster just by delegating correctly.

WAYS TO STOP PUNISHING YOUR BEST ASSOCIATES

One possible solution is to reduce the billable hour requirements your associates need to gain eligibility for a bonus. That's right, reduce it! That is their reward for hard work. If every associate needs to bill 1,800 hours before he or she is eligible for a bonus, consider lowering the bonus for your star associates to 1,700 or 1,600 hours. Most firm managers haven't figured out (or don't care) that this method allows your best associates to make more money faster *and* work fewer hours. Perhaps you're thinking, "How is this good for profitability?" Avoiding the enormous costs of hiring and training associates to replace departing associates should be reason enough.

Reducing associates' billable hour requirement could also reduce associate churn. If adopting incentives that reward top associates reduced churn 10 percent and caused them to stay at your firm and remain productive, would you do it? Most firms would say yes. Why? Because losing one top associate is like losing one and a half or two average associates. Another critical issue to consider is the fact that clients hate associate churn, perhaps more than you do.

Other options to keep your top associates include putting them on an accelerated fast-track to partner. This idea is fraught with peril, and while your partners are fighting over the merits of doing it, your best associates are leaving in droves. Another possible solution is to reward associates with their own coaches. More firms are hiring personal coaches to work with their associates. It's positioned as a reward for the associate and a way for the firm to show its investment in that associate's long-term future with the firm. Associates love it, and it creates a stronger bond between associates and the firm. And if having a coach makes an associate more profitable and a better performer, you might consider providing coaches for those you don't think are the best.

Another thing you can do to keep your best associates is to give them more choices on challenging work. Many firms think they do this, but that is not what we've observed. The partner with the biggest book of business is more likely to dictate the kind of work these top associates receive. Don't *presume* what an associate wants! Ask! If you ask great associates whether they've ever been asked for feedback on the type of work they want, most will laugh in your face. We can't stress strongly enough how important it is to communicate with associates.

Many firms are losing their best associates at a greater rate than ever as a result of the unintended punishment mentioned in this chapter. If you don't do anything to address the issue, unfulfilled and overworked associates will vote with their feet and leave the firm. They may go in-house or move on to another firm. Either way, your precious resource will be gone. The saddest part is that their departure is preventable in many cases.

Coaching is a motivational tool more powerful than money.

┌─────┐
│ 43 │
└─────┘

MOTIVATING OTHERS TO MARKET

HOW CAN WE CREATE A SELF-PROPELLED MARKETING CULTURE?

Firm leaders often ask how they can motivate others to get into the marketing game because they want as many as possible to pull their weight. The simple truth is that *you* can't motivate others. *They* must motivate themselves. You may use external motivators, but they won't have a lasting impact on someone's behavior. Only internal motivation has a lasting effect. Leaders who use only external motivation will wear themselves out and have poor results to show for it.

CREATE AN ENVIRONMENT THAT PROMOTES MARKETING

Gifted leaders infuse their firm cultures with an overriding sense of meaning and purpose that allows the motivation inherent in all of us to surface. Most people are inherently motivated by a higher purpose. Bringing more dollars in the door isn't a higher purpose, yet nearly every firm we come in contact with seems to have that as its purpose in one form or another. These firms do nothing to tap into the innate motivation possessed by everyone in the firm. Extremely rare is the leader who creates an environment in which everyone is pursuing a shared higher purpose.

At the very least, leaders should create an environment that doesn't tacitly or overtly promote fear. Fear can take myriad forms: fear of being ridiculed, fear of failure, and fear of looking incompetent, to name a few. The list is nearly endless. Motivation occurs naturally in all of us when fear doesn't dominate our thinking. Unfortunately, many compensation systems unintentionally act as de-motivators by promoting fear. As a firm leader, be vigilant about doing anything that interferes with natural motivation!

In addition to creating the right environment, leaders can do two other things to promote a self-propelled marketing culture: (1) model the behavior they want others to achieve and (2) provide instruction in excruciating detail on *how* to undertake the marketing activities they want others to exhibit (not a skill set supplied in most firms). Nothing is more likely to motivate professionals than the entire executive team modeling great marketing behaviors.

A book written almost 25 years ago by Ferdinand Fournies,[1] *Coaching for Improved Work Performance*, contains great insights on motivation. Fournies finds it preposterous when a leader or manager discovers an employee's nonperformance (for example, not doing any marketing) and reacts by modifying the compensation system to create incentives for the employee to improve performance. He found that, in most cases, the real reason for nonperformance was that the employee didn't know *how* to do it. If that's true, you are much better off investing in a skills development program that addresses the "hows" of the process.

Our experience reinforces Fournies' conclusion. Even when someone knows how to do something, if the how is inconsistent with her style, approach, or personality, she won't do it.

Sometimes firms hire us with the hope that we will motivate others to do marketing, which, as stated earlier, isn't possible. The truth is, many people avoid marketing functions because they simply don't know how to approach them. For the professionals who lack know-how, coaching can pay large dividends. In most cases, that's exactly what non-rainmakers need — someone to show them how.

WHAT MOTIVATES PEOPLE TO MARKET

One highly overrated and overused motivational tool is money. Partners who already earn a comfortable income aren't likely to be motivated by money. And money won't motivate people to excel in something they don't know how to do. In these cases, offering more money will only increase the person's level of discomfort, not his performance.

INCREASE MOTIVATION; FIND LOTS OF REASONS FOR MARKETING

Let's assume that people do know how to market. Then what? Many people know that, left to their own devices, they will do what they are accustomed to: practicing law, tending to business, etc. If you have some desire to improve your marketing, the best way to stay motivated is to find as many reasons as possible for doing it. The more reasons you have for doing something, the more motivation you'll have for doing it.

For example, if you have sixteen reasons to undertake marketing, you are less likely to experience a dip in motivation. Should you come up short on one of those reasons, you have another fifteen reasons why you should do it. And when motivation does dip, you won't fall as deeply into a funk and you will bounce back more quickly.

You might ask, "In addition to money, what reasons are there to market?" Your list of answers might include:

- Increased prestige and power within the firm

- Increased prestige within the business community

- Increased power in the firm

- Developing business you love to do, rather than business for the sake of money

- Better relationships with clients, co-workers , and partners

- More rewarding connections and influence in the community

- Feeling successful

- Greater control over your own destiny

Remember, your list of motivators is very personal and may be unlike anyone else's in the world. If the list is short, give thought to other reasons why you're doing what you're doing. Take all the time you need to develop your list.

In the final analysis, all of the external reasons in the world won't prove as enduring as one simple internal motivator — you do what you do because you love doing it. In the movie *Field of Dreams*, Ray Liotta (as Shoeless Joe Jackson) tells the character played by Kevin Costner that he loved baseball so much he'd have "played for nothing." In our opinion, *that* is the most enduring kind of motivation. It's also the kind of motivation possessed by your best rainmakers. People derive meaning from the activity itself. While the number of people in your firm with that mindset may be low, there is plenty more that your firm can do to get others into the marketing game.

Being a model for collaboration is better than advocating for it.

$$\boxed{44}$$

MAKING COLLABORATION HAPPEN

How Can I Model Collaboration?

We have many clients who are continually talking about wanting more collaboration from their partners. Firm leaders and managers can help create a self-propelled marketing culture when they model behavior they want others to achieve. Perhaps the best way to show how modeling can work is by example.

One of our Canadian clients serves as the practice group leader of the environmental practice group. She sponsored a mini conference that brought together clients, prospects, all of her firm's environmental lawyers, and firm lawyers from other practice areas. This initiative was successful and tightened the relationships within the practice group.

This lawyer is the kind of person our coaches love to work with because she saw everything about this mini conference as a chance to collaborate and help others succeed. She rose to the challenge in several ways:

1. With the help of her marketing department, she sent formal invitations to clients and prospective clients.

2. She personally phoned to invite clients and prospective clients.

3. She personally phoned to invite her partners in other practice areas.

4. She invited out-of-town partners and associates she doesn't see very often.

5. As the day of the event drew closer, she sent periodic reminder e-mails to generate excitement among her partners.

6. She sent out several reminders with clear responsibilities for those with assigned roles.

7. She arranged a dinner that brought together her partners and associates, and another dinner that created relationships between firm lawyers and clients.

8. She arranged a group meeting to coordinate the anticipated follow-up to be done after the event.

9. She arranged monthly follow-up reporting by group members on their follow-up with clients and prospects.

All of these things led to a great turnout and increased the level of personal connection among clients, prospects, and lawyers. It also led to better connections among her partners and had the effect of generating many more connections between her clients and partners. Finally, it led to several mandates for new work. Perhaps the highest compliment was delivered to her in the form of a request by management to do the same thing in other cities.

Doing all of this took time for a person who was already very busy. Nevertheless, you get out of these events what you put into them. Many professionals *talk* about collaboration, but very few are able to *do* it. This client was able to be a model for collaboration — something all too rarely seen.

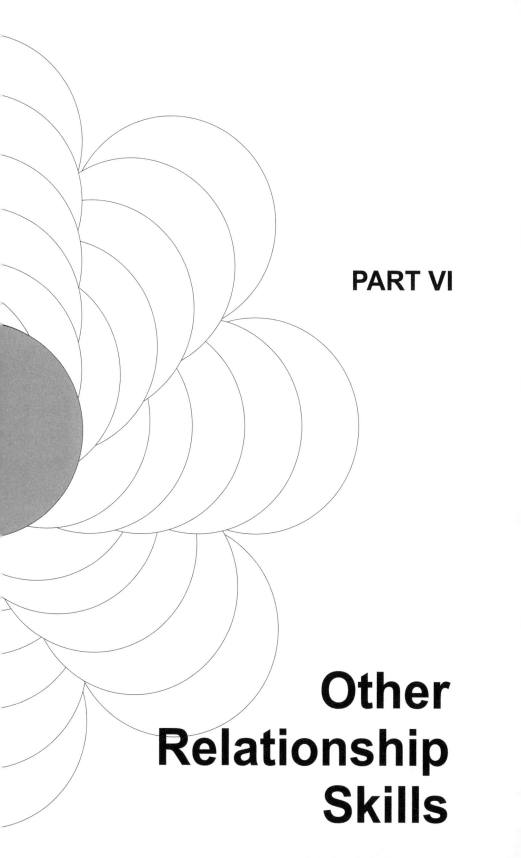

PART VI

Other
Relationship
Skills

Hiring talented people is crucial to staying competitive in today's marketplace. Make sure you know where to look for them.

45

FINDING TOP LATERAL TALENT

WHAT MUST NOT BE OVERLOOKED TO STAY COMPETITIVE?

Competition for winning and keeping clients has never been more intense. The same is true for finding exceptional talent. We find that many firms have very focused programs for recruiting young professionals out of college, law school, or business school. Recruiting experienced laterals is a valuable approach to growing your firm, but most firms have nebulous procedures in place or leave recruitment to their managing partners. Add to this the revolving door of associates going in-house and seasoned professionals being wooed to other firms, and recruitment quickly rises to the top of a firm's ongoing problems.

In today's marketplace, your clients are not likely to wait for your firm to land the right talent. Because the greatest asset in all professional services firms is people, everyone in the firm is responsible for attracting good people. If they're not, you could be in trouble.

Here are eight ideas you can use to improve your chances of finding exceptional talent to stay competitive:

1. INSPIRE EVERYONE ON YOUR TEAM TO LOOK FOR TOP TALENT. Recruitment at the level your clients demand can't be done by just a few people. Don't leave it up to the recruiting coordinator, human resources, managing partner, or practice group leader. Partners, associates, and assistants talk with people in their business every day. The key words here are "inspire" and "everyone." Consider offering a financial incentive if the firm hires and keeps someone for a year or more. Your relationship with your team members will determine the level of inspiration they devote to the task of finding top talent.

2. ALWAYS LOOK FOR TOP TALENT. The best at hiring are thinking about the next hire constantly.

3. USE THE FULL POWER OF YOUR NETWORK. Try to think outside your personal network. Ask your clients, colleagues, friends, and family for referrals and ideas for candidates. One lawyer we coached was looking for additional associates and asked his client about talented associates she worked with from other firms. When a colleague of mine interviews candidates, he routinely asks who they think is the best in their field. Your network is a rich resource for recruiting talent.

4. TURN TO EXISTING LATERALS FOR INFORMATION. Existing lateral hires who have worked well for the firm hold valuable information about other professionals from their former firms. Talk to them about potential candidates and assess why the lateral hire was a success.

5. BE CREATIVE TO FIND THE BEST CANDIDATES. Instead of wooing the best partner from down the street, consider hiring the best associate.

6. THINK LONG TERM AND BE PERSISTENT. It might take several years to land top talent. In one case, an executive tried calling a desirable candidate several times before he even received a return phone call. Then it took several calls over many months before the candidate would consider meeting with him. Eventually, this

executive succeeded in hiring his targeted talent from a competing company.

7. BUILD A RELATIONSHIP WITH THE CANDIDATE. Building a relationship reveals insights about a candidate, her practice, and the possibility of good chemistry to ensure a good fit for the firm. A lateral candidate with significant economic clout can be so attractive you might want to hire her quickly. There's no need to rush into the interviewing process, which tends to focus on making a good impression.

8. WATCH THE COMPETITION. Watch your competition's movement for potential hiring opportunities. These could come after a key partner leaves the firm or with a change in management. You can also find opportunities in tracking a competing attorney who consistently wins litigation cases for clients in a specific industry — one you want to penetrate. Many firms have marketing departments or librarians who can access industry databases to help you track your competition.

Are you looking for a lateral professional right now? Whom can you call first for a referral? Have you been courting a candidate but given up on her? Why not call her right now?

Recruiting top talent is too important to overlook. Don't give up. Learn to be vigilant and inspire those around you to be, too. Lateral hiring opportunities are closer than you think.

If you hate selling, get your clients to do some of the selling
for you through third-party endorsements.

┌─────┐
│ 46 │
└─────┘

THIRD-PARTY ENDORSEMENTS

CAN MY CLIENTS HELP ME SELL?

We don't know many professional services firms that attempt to have their clients do their selling for them. Every other business has long ago harnessed the power of a third-party endorsement as one of the finest ways to generate new business. Some professionals are concerned about ethics violations, with lawyers being among the most skittish. In our view, every professional can and should harness the power of third-party endorsements without running afoul of the ethics police. It can be a very effective differentiator, particularly if your competitors are hesitant about putting endorsements to work.

Endorsements can be written or verbal, which usually means by telephone. Our preference is to have both. The written ones ought to be on your firm's website so that visitors there know what others are saying about you.

SECURING WRITTEN TESTIMONIALS

1. BE SURE YOUR CLIENTS ARE SATISFIED. Solicit feedback on a regular basis from your favorite clients. Don't wait until the end of

an engagement to ask. In some cases, it makes sense to ask for feedback at milestones along the way. Simple questions can include: "How have we done?" "How have we been doing?" "What have you liked about our work?" "How do we compare to the other professionals you deal with?" Just remember that, if you don't ask, you won't receive. More importantly, your chances of securing an endorsement from an unsatisfied client are nil. While you're seeking endorsements by asking these questions, you're also doing something far more important — you're ensuring that your client's needs and expectations are met.

2. CAPTURE THEIR VERBAL COMMENTS AND REDUCE THEM TO WRITING. If the client gushes about you while answering your questions, this becomes your opening to ask about a testimonial. If you listen carefully to what he or she says, you can usually excerpt directly from the comments.

Ask to use the person's comments on your firm's website and in other marketing materials. Usually the client is flattered. Most times she is grateful if *you* take the responsibility to write up what she said and send it to her for approval rather than asking her to create something.

Send your client a very short e-mail renewing your request, thank him for agreeing to help, and include the exact language you heard him use. One or two sentences is plenty. In fact, it's much better than one or two paragraphs. All you want is something very short and to the point. Here's an example:

John,

What follows is a write-up I would like to use in my marketing materials (including my website) with your permission. It was crafted in large part from my notes from our conversation. Please feel free to change it or modify it as you see fit so it sounds like you. Thanks in advance for your willingness to help. It's greatly appreciated.

Warm regards,

Mark

3. IT ONLY TAKES ONE ENDORSEMENT TO HAVE AN IMPACT. Bill, a career management consultant, received a holiday card from a very satisfied client who gushed about Bill's work and how, as a result of Bill's help, he made $600,000 in his second year in business. Bill showed this card to a prospective client and the prospect signed up for Bill's program on the spot.

4. GATHER PLENTY OF TESTIMONIALS. How many testimonials should you accumulate? There is no hard-and-fast rule, but you want as many as you can get! One is better than none. Five are better than one or two, and dozens are even better. If you are delighting your clients regularly, you should be able to accumulate several dozen testimonials in several months.

Testimonials can be particularly valuable when you are trying to develop the client's confidence in your junior people. If you can get a third party to verify that your junior professionals are outstanding, it can go a long way toward eliminating the resistance you might otherwise face when transitioning work to them. Once you've accumulated favorable comments from clients about your team, you can send these comments to prospective clients who are reluctant to work with anyone other than you.

5. IF ENDORSEMENTS ARE NOT PERMITTED, SEE WHETHER CLIENTS WILL SERVE AS REFERENCES. If you can't persuade your firm to gather written testimonials, at the very least see whether your best clients will serve as references. That way, when prospective clients ask you questions like, "Why should we hire you?" you can respond by saying, "We encourage you to talk to our clients and ask them that question."

If you are the overly cautious type, you could test the waters first. The clients who agree to serve as verbal references can be quizzed BY YOU on how they might respond to prospective client inquiries. Ask a simple question like, "If a prospective client called and asked about your experience in dealing with our firm, what might you say?" This is best done after you've gathered feedback and you're satisfied that your client will be complimentary. Then you can list him or her as a reference with great confidence, always with permission, of course.

The best professionals have the largest stable of delighted clients and can easily use third-party endorsements as a distinct competitive advantage. Remember to tilt the playing field in your favor. Testimonials are one very effective way to do that.

Hiring a great coach can deliver a significant return on your firm's investment.

┌─────┐
│ 47 │
└─────┘

HIRING A GREAT COACH

How Can I Tell the Difference Between a Great Coach and a Good One?

We've noticed a dramatic increase in firms wanting to use coaches to develop and refine their people's skills. Given the considerable increase in demand for coaches, many consulting firms and other people with little or no formal coaching experience or training are jumping on the coaching bandwagon. The risks of making a poor hiring decision internally (a chief marketing officer with coaching skills) or externally (hiring a coach) have increased because of the flood of people who now call themselves coaches.

Just because someone calls himself a coach doesn't make him one. The flip side is also true, as some consultants do exhibit effective coaching behaviors. This presents a challenge for your firm's management as a prospective buyer of coaching services. Don't make the label an issue. We would rather you hire a consultant who exhibits coaching behaviors than a coach who exhibits consulting behaviors.

Consultants are now offering coaching because it's what people want. Be very wary of yesterday's consultant claiming to be today's coach. There is a very definite place for consultants if that is what your firm needs. It makes sense to hire a consultant if you want to do some strategic planning, launch a branding campaign, analyze your firm's compensation system, or do some organizational design and development.

DIFFERENCES BETWEEN A COACH AND A CONSULTANT

Although there is no bright line test to distinguish between a coach and a consultant, there are some helpful indicators. A disproportionate number of coaches work with one person at a time. And it is individuals, not firms, who hire them. While that is typically true, it is not always the case. For example, we are hired by some firms to develop an individual's skills, and we are hired by other firms to work with groups.

Consultants are viewed as experts who make recommendations or offer opinions and advice as a first resort, whereas coaches inquire and ask lots of insightful questions to draw upon what their clients already know. They are adept at drawing out *your* internal wisdom to help you solve problems and arrive at specific, practical, concrete steps on *how* to move your skills to the next level.

With rare exceptions, consultants will put more energy into giving advice. And the advice they give is focused more on *what* to do rather than *how* to do it. For example, the mere fact that you know you should contact a former employee of your best client to expand your network does not mean you'd know how to begin the conversation if you did call her. A good coach helps you to commit to calling within a specific time frame and may even ask you to be clear about whether you intend to make contact by e-mail or by phone. In addition, a coach is more likely to help you rehearse how you will handle the first 30 seconds of that call (if that is where you are experiencing difficulty). Coaches will also close the loop to find out how the call turned out.

Coaches will give advice, but only *after* they are sure you don't possess your own ideas for solving the problem. Once they see you are stuck, they provide customized, unit-of-one advice that works for you. Coaches are also interested in understanding your motivation for doing something and in knowing that it suits your personality or that it seems to be far outside your comfort zone. Their insights are highly customized and practical. They collaborate with you to help you understand your situation and to discover solutions you can implement.

Consultants are sometimes hired solely for their planning expertise. Coaches go light on planning and put more energy into encouraging clients to execute. If you want help keeping the promises you make to yourself, then hire a coach. Coaches are skilled at helping you to keep your commitments to yourself and to follow through.

Coaches go out of their way to reinforce the lessons you are learning. If you are doing something effectively, your coach will heavily reinforce that behavior so you will keep doing it. For example, if you routinely visit at least one client at his place of business each quarter, your coach might say, "That is a great practice. Keep doing it!" The good ones will even ask how or why you decided to adopt such a sound practice. Consultants often won't even know you visit one client per quarter and therefore can't reinforce that positive behavior.

There is always a gap between what we know and what we do. Just think about the diet you are on or the exercise you were going to do this morning. We know what to do, but we don't always do it! A coach will help you narrow the gap between knowing and doing.

To reinforce positive behaviors, coaches talk with you regularly two or three times each month. Consultants do most of their work in person and are on airplanes a great deal of the time. One quick way to distinguish a successful consultant from a successful coach is to ask how many days she travelled to clients for on-site visits recently. A safe general rule is that those who are out more than six days per month are probably consultants, not coaches. Our coaches are in very high demand, but we rarely travel more than six days per month. By contrast, a consultant who is in very high demand might be out of his office ten or twenty days per month.

Coaches often help you become aware of old habits and beliefs that are holding you back. Consultants are more likely to add new knowledge. Coaches are great at uncovering old or outworn beliefs that stop you from applying this new knowledge. One example of an old belief that stops people from getting better at business generation is "It's rude to ask questions." If you believe that, no amount of exhortation from experts will convince you to start using questions in your approach to business development.

Telling the Great Coaches from the Good Ones

How do you tell the great coaches from the good ones? Here's a list:

Passion. Great coaches genuinely love the work they do and want other people to find their own passion.

Good references. Be sure to rigorously check references. If the coach you want to hire can't provide references, especially references from your industry, proceed with caution. References will rave about great coaches.

A proven system is used. We use The Maraia Method®[1] in two different ways. First, we provide our clients with a framework for approaching common, everyday situations faced by everyone in the relationship-building process. This actually diminishes the need for coaches over time and encourages people to do things for themselves.

Second, our coaches use The Maraia Method® to follow up with clients. There are a dozen things about our coaching method that make it unique and highly effective. Two trademark services our coaches provide include (1) initiating many of the calls so that full value is received and (2) conducting debriefing calls *after* clients have taken action. We find adults learn far more if they reflect on what happened.

Can pass a simulated coaching situation. During the interview process with a coach, consider simulating a real situation — in effect, a mock coaching session. This quickly exposes people who can talk a good game, but can't do it well. One client in

Toronto wanted to hire a marketing director who had strong coaching skills. Management had narrowed the field down to two candidates. Both candidates seemed equally qualified, but when the marketing partner put both candidates through a simulated coaching scenario, it became clear that one was far better at coaching. This same test can also be used with outside providers. The more varied the simulations, the more easily you can determine who possesses the best coaching skills.

GREAT COACHES CARE. Perhaps the one intangible that differentiates the greatest coaches is their genuine concern for the people with whom they work. During the interview process, pay close attention to whether the coach you are considering sees things in you that you can't see in yourself. That will inspire your confidence in his vision.

We genuinely want our readers to make the right decision on the coaches they hire, whether as inside or outside providers. If you follow the guidelines set forth in this chapter, we believe you will make a better hiring decision and find the coach who is right for you.

Setting daily or weekly metrics can dramatically
increase your results.

┌─────────┐
│   48   │
└─────────┘

SETTING METRICS AND TARGETS

HOW CAN I IMPROVE MY MARKETING EFFORTS
USING METRICS?

Metrics are important in every endeavor. The phrase "You only value what you measure" is as applicable to marketing as to other aspects of your practice. Nearly all professionals use billable hours as a metric to measure how productive they are. If firms were as diligent in setting marketing metrics, you'd see much better performance in the marketing arena. In our work with clients, we've noticed dramatic improvements in an individual's marketing performance when she is operating with a clear set of measurable goals or metrics.

You can set metrics for the year, the month, the week, or for an event. I would suggest setting weekly metrics when feasible so that you can frequently assess how you're doing.

The key to setting effective metrics is that they must be realistic, personalized, and fun. If you don't set realistic targets, you will most likely become discouraged and revert to what you know best, which is to practice your trade.

It's best to start with modest goals and gradually build up to more ambitious ones, rather than to start out too ambitiously. A realistic target might be to make one marketing-related phone call — one that isn't very personalized — a day. Marketing goals also need to be personalized so that the person setting the goal actually *wants* to achieve it. To personalize that "one marketing call per day" further, you might consider reaching out to one dormant client per day. If one call per day is too ambitious, try making a call every other day, or even once a week for the really marketing challenged. Just start somewhere.

Personalization is critical for a number of reasons. If you hate public speaking, it hardly makes sense to set a metric of doing one speaking engagement per quarter. If you *do* like public speaking, then additional metrics can be developed for each speaking engagement. For example, you might set a metric of calling five clients or former clients before each speaking engagement. You can also set another metric following the talk. For example, make three follow-up calls to people who attended your presentation.

One of our clients had developed an international reputation doing litigation for doctors. He was burned out practicing law and wanted to start his own consulting practice targeted on that same group of doctors. He is still practicing law, but he is finding it very hard to bill seven to eight hours every day the way he did when he was younger. His coach pointed out that he will continue to find cranking out billable hours much harder because his heart's not in it. With the help of his coach, he devised a set of personalized metrics to measure his progress in developing his consulting practice. He created the following metrics:

1. Make three marketing-related calls per week to doctors who are part of his network to gather market research about his proposed service offering and to set meetings.

2. Set three marketing-related meetings a month from among that same group.

Now that he has metrics established, he can measure his weekly progress against those metrics. Keep in mind that setting a metric like "make three phone calls per week to dormant clients" isn't enough if you don't have a clear idea about the purpose for each call. However, with the metric in place and clarity about the purpose for each call, you will achieve amazing results.

Here are some metrics on goals our clients have set for themselves:

- Move 25 boxes of old files out of my office in the next three months.

- Increase circulation of my electronic update from 150 subscribers to 300 subscribers in the next year.

- Have my assistant put my written list of 200 contacts into an electronic format.

- Write down three marketing successes per week in my marketing diary.

- Meet with or call one new prospective client each week.

- Add one new target client to my network each week.

- Call five dormant clients before my talk on December 2 to invite them to my presentation.

- Make one free, on-site client visit each quarter.

- Solicit feedback from one client each month.

- Call my three best referral sources once per month and offer to be a sounding board.

- Meet with referral sources once every other month.

- Delegate 20 hours' worth of leasing work to my associate this week.

- Meet with one litigator each week to find out more about his or her ideal client.

- Call one dormant client per week to reconnect.

- Distribute a written agenda at each monthly team meeting.

If this works out as hoped, you are likely to achieve the metric you want. When that happens, set more aggressive milestones each time one milestone has been achieved, and watch your marketing productivity take off.

END NOTES

CHAPTER 4

1. For more on speaking and writing, see Chapter 34, "Using Speaking to Win New Clients," and Chapter 36, "Making Publications Pay Off," in *Rainmaking Made Simple: What Every Professional Must Know*, by Mark M. Maraia.

CHAPTER 6

1. Learn more about preparing for presentations in Chapter 35, "The Secrets of a Winning Presentation," in *Rainmaking Made Simple: What Every Professional Must Know*, by Mark M. Maraia.

CHAPTER 16

1. *Forbes*, May 7, 2007.

2. Lincoln's first inaugural address. www.bartleby.com

CHAPTER 36

1. "First seek to understand, then to be understood." Habit 5 from Stephen R. Covey's *Seven Habits of Highly Effective People*. (1989). New York: Simon & Schuster.

CHAPTER 43

1. Fournies, F. (2000). *Coaching for Improved Work Performance* (rev. ed.). New York: McGraw-Hill.

CHAPTER 47

1. The Maraia Method® is both a process for improving selling behaviors through the deepening of relationships and a process for refining coaching behaviors. Working with thousands of clients over nineteen years has allowed us to hone this into a results-oriented structure that is motivational as well as transformational. The fundamentals of our approach are:

- Allow the person to assess his or her own performance.

- Focus on the strengths of the individual.

- Stress personal accountability and self-awareness as goals.

- Encourage specificity and detail through keen observation.

- Focus on one or two new actions or behaviors the individual is willing to initiate.

- Assess the probability of a new action or behavior happening; then increase the odds of that happening.

- Receive specific time and date commitments, and calendar the desired action.

- Perform near real-time follow-up as to the success of the action.

- Provide detailed and behavior-based feedback.

- Allow the individual to assimilate what was learned and the benefit of the new behaviors.

- Increase the number, frequency, and depth of conversations with the individual.

RECOMMENDED READING

Anonymous. (2007). *A Course in Miracles*. Mill Valley, CA: Foundation for Inner Peace.

Ariely, Dan. (2008). *Predictably Irrational: The Hidden Forces That Shape Our Decisions*. New York: HarperCollins.

Calagione, Sam. (2005). *Brewing Up a Business: Adventures in Entrepreneurship from the Founder of Dogfish Head Craft Brewery*. Hoboken, NJ: John Wiley & Sons.

Conley, Chip. (2007). *Peak: How Great Companies Get Their Mojo from Maslow*. San Francisco, CA: Jossey-Bass.

Covey, Stephen R. (2004). *Stephen R. Covey Live — The 8th Habit — From Effectiveness to Greatness*. New York: Simon & Schuster.

Covey, Stephen M.R. (2006). *The SPEED of Trust: The One Thing That Changes Everything*. New York: Free Press.

Goldsmith, Marshall. (2007). *What Got You Here Won't Get You There: How Successful People Become Even More Successful*. New York: Hyperion.

Maraia, Mark M. (2003). *Rainmaking Made Simple: What Every Professional Must Know*. Littleton, CO: Professional Services Publishing.

Nour, David. (2008). *Relationship Economics: Transform Your Most Valuable Business Contacts into Personal and Professional Success*. Hoboken, NJ: John Wiley & Sons.

Salacuse, Jeswald W. (2006). *Leading Leaders: How to Manage Smart, Talented, Rich, and Powerful People*. New York: AMACOM.

Snider, Debra. (2003). *The Productive Culture Blueprint*. Chicago: American Bar Association Career Resource Center.

Snyder, Tom, & Kearns, Kevin. (2008). *Escaping the Price-Driven Sale: How World-Class Sellers Create Extraordinary Profit*. New York: McGraw-Hill.

The Arbinger Institute. (2002). *Leadership and Self-Deception: Getting Out of the Box*. San Francisco, CA: Berrett-Koehler.

Thompson, Gregg, & Biro, Susanne. (2007). *Unleashed! Expecting Greatness and Other Secrets of Coaching for Exceptional Performance*. New York: Select Books.

Zander, Rosamund Stone. (2000). *The Art of Possibility: Transforming Professional and Personal Life*. New York: Penguin Group.

INDEX

collaboration:
  modeling to increase partner, 179–180
  splitting billing credit following, 155–156

colleagues:
  asking for a commitment from your, 148
  coaching skills applied to conversations with, 151–153
  learning from, 9
  questions to help you connect with, 141–143
  splitting billing credit with, 155–156, 167
  See also partners; rainmakers

communication:
  e-mail, 16
  telephone calls and voicemail, 13–15
  triage approach to handling client, 95–97

competing firms:
  keeping your clients away from, 71
  nine ideas for dealing with, 71–74

connecting. *See* relationship building

consultants, 192–194

contact list:
  calling your, 11
  prioritizing your, 11–12

Costner, Kevin, 178

CSO (client satisfaction officers), 79–80

curiosity:
  being intentional with your, 45
  description of, 43–44
  rewards of, 44–45

D

decision-makers:
  five guidelines for meeting, 18–19
  reasons to meet, 17
  treating everyone as a, 19–20

delegating work:
  avoiding burnout by, 59
  marketing meeting preparation to associates, 166
  obstacles to effective practice of, 119–122
  pitfalls and benefits of, 127
  steps to effectively, 123–127
  telephone calls to assistant, 95–97
  See also assistants

delegation steps:
  1. decide what work you want to delegate, 123–124
  2. determining best person to handle this project, 124
  3. identify the goal of the project, 125–126
  4. establishing clear milestones and deadlines, 126
  5. have a protocol for potential problems, 126
  6. give your associate clear feedback, 126
  7. check with associate on lessons learned, 127

E

e-mail communication, 16

F

Field of Dreams (film), 178

firms:
  avoiding associate churn at, 171–173
  creating marketing culture at, 175–178, 179–180
  finding top lateral talent, 183–185
  keeping your clients away from larger, 71
  nine ideas when competing with large, 71–74
  rainmaker development at, 165–170
  See also partners; professional practices

RELATIONSHIPS ARE EVERYTHING!

"how can I help?" mindset to, 137–138

marketing meeting opportunities for, 21–24

quality of interactions and, 106

questions to help you connect with partners, 141–143

raising your internal profile for, 135–139

re-igniting your curiosity for, 43–45

robust network outcome of, 2

with service provider colleagues, 9

See also marketing; Networking; Networks

relationship literacy, 2

relationships:
as focus of mission, 1–2

note-taking to gain advantage in, 91–93

releasing negative emotions to protect, 53–55

triage approach to handling calls to improve, 95–97

Relationships Are Everything! (Maraia), 3

S

scarcity mindset/thinking, 33–34

sharing kudos and credit, 138

Simmons, Cleat, 157

splitting billing credit:
appropriate times for, 155–156

benefits of, 156

as rainmaker development strategy, 167

staff generated leads, 10

SunGard Higher Education Managed Services, 157

T

talent:
eight ideas for finding exceptional, 184–185

importance of effective, 183

team credibility building, 99–101

telephone calls:
leaving voicemail messages, 13–15

prioritizing your contact list for, 11–12

triage approach to handling, 95–97

third-party endorsements:
asking for, 74

capturing client comments for, 188

gathering as many as possible, 189

importance of even single, 189

references instead of, 189–190

securing written, 187–188

trust:
abundance mentality to build, 34–35

inspiring client confidence and, 87–90

U

unreturned messages:
effective voicemail message to avoid, 15

how to respond to, 14

V

vacations, 59–60

value:
determining what clients want, 84–85

determining your role in delivering, 83–84

examining/modifying your business practices to deliver, 85–86

voicemail messages:
common-sense protocols for leaving, 13–14

elements of an effective, 15

"friendly persistence" approach to leaving, 16

when to use e-mail instead of, 16

W

RELATIONSHIPS ARE EVERYTHING!

THE AUTHOR

Mark Maraia is a widely respected business coach, trainer, and thought leader in the professional services field whose mission is to increase relationship literacy in the business world. He is the author of *Rainmaking Made Simple: What Every Professional Must Know*. Many professionals consider *Rainmaking Made Simple* to be the definitive "how to" field guide on business development. The ideas presented in Maraia's books have been field-tested many times over by thousands of professionals and have helped them develop relationship-building skills without compromising integrity or professional status. By his writing and coaching, Mark has helped clients achieve significant bottom-line results. He also publishes an opt-in electronic newsletter that is followed by nearly 4,000 people in 70 countries.

You may contact Mark at http://www.markmaraia.com.